Rosencrantz and Guildenstern Are Dead

Tom Stoppard's other plays include *Jumpers, Travesties* (Tony Award), *Night and Day, After Magritte, The Real Thing* (Tony Award), *Enter A Free Man, Hapgood,* and *Indian Ink* (a stage adaptation of his own radio play, *In the Native State*), *Arcadia* (Olivier Award and the Critics Award) and *The Invention of Love* (which won him his seventh Evening Standard Award for his plays).

His radio plays include: *If You're Glad I'll Be Frank, Albert's Bridge* (Italia Prize), *Where Are They Now?, Artist Descending A Staircase, The Dog It Was That Died, In the Native State* (Sony Award).

Work for television includes: *Professional Foul* (Bafta Award, Broadcasting Press Guild Award). His film credits include *Rosencrantz and Guildenstern Are Dead*, which he also directed (winner of the Golden Lion, Venice Film Festival). He also co-authored *Shakespeare In Love* with Marc Norman (Academy Award for Best Screenplay).

TOM STOPPARD

Rosencrantz and Guildenstern Are Dead

faber and faber
LONDON·NEW YORK

First published in 1967
by Faber and Faber Limited
3 Queen Square London WC1N 3AU
This paperback edition first published in 1968
Reset in 2000

Photoset by Parker Typesetting Service, Leicester
Printed in England by Mackays of Chatham PLC
All rights reserved

28 30 29

The first major production of *Rosencrantz and Guildenstern Are Dead* was first performed by the Royal National Theatre on 11 April 1967. The cast was as follows:

Rosencrantz John Stride
Guildenstern Edward Petherbridge
The Player Graham Crowden
Players Alan Adams, Oliver Cotton, Neil Fitzpatrick, Luke Hardy, Roger Kemp
Hamlet John McEnery
Ophelia Caroline John
Claudius Kenneth Mackintosh
Gertrude Mary Griffiths
Polonius Peter Cellier
Fortinbras David Bailie
Horatio David Hargreaves
Ambassador David Ryall
Courtiers and Attendants David Bailie, Petronella Barker, David Belcher, Margo Cunningham, Denis de Marne, Kay Gailie, Reginald Green, David Hargreaves, William Hobbs, Richard Kay, Lee Menzies, Leonard Pearce, Ron Pember, Frederick Pyne, Maggie Riley, David Ryall, Christopher Timothy
Player-Musicians Lawrence Kennedy (flute), Laurie Morgan (drums), Stephen Nagy (oboe),
Offstage Musicians Malcolm Hall, Edward Wilson

Directed by Derek Goldby
Designed by Desmond Healey

Lighting by Richard Pilbrow
Music and sound effects by Marc Wilkinson

The action takes place within and around the action of
Hamlet.

Act One

Two Elizabethans passing the time in a place without any visible character.

They are well dressed – hats, cloaks, sticks and all.

Each of them has a large leather money bag.

Guildenstern's bag is nearly empty.

Rosencrantz's bag is nearly full.

The reason being: they are betting on the toss of a coin, in the following manner: Guildenstern (hereafter 'Guil') takes a coin out of his bag, spins it, letting it fall. Rosencrantz (hereafter 'Ros') studies it, announces it as 'heads' (as it happens) and puts it into his own bag. Then they repeat the process. They have apparently been doing this for some time.

The run of 'heads' is impossible, yet Ros betrays no surprise at all – he feels none. However, he is nice enough to feel a little embarrassed at taking so much money off his friend. Let that be his character note.

Guil is well alive to the oddity of it. He is not worried about the money, but he is worried by the implications; aware but not going to panic about it – his character note.

Guil sits. Ros stands (he does the moving, retrieving coins).

Guil spins. Ros studies coin.

Ros Heads.

He picks it up and puts it in his bag. The process is repeated.

Heads.

Again.

Heads.

Again.

Heads.

Again.

Heads.

Guil (*flipping a coin*) There is an art to the building up of suspense.

Ros Heads.

Guil (*flipping another*) Though it can be done by luck alone.

Ros Heads.

Guil If that's the word I'm after.

Ros (*raises his head at Guil*) Seventy-six love.

Guil gets up but has nowhere to go. He spins another coin over his shoulder without looking at it, his attention being directed at his environment or lack of it.

Heads.

Guil A weaker man might be moved to re-examine his faith, if in nothing else at least in the law of probability.

He flips a coin over his shoulder as he goes to look upstage.

Ros Heads.

Guil, examining the confines of the stage, flips over two more coins as he does so, one by one of course. Ros announces each of them as 'heads'.

Guil (*musing*) The law of probability, it has been oddly asserted, is something to do with the proposition that if six monkeys (*He has surprised himself.*) . . . if six monkeys were . . .

Ros Game?

Guil Were they?

Ros Are you?

Guil (*understanding*) Game. (*Flips a coin.*) The law of averages, if I have got this right, means that if six monkeys were thrown up in the air for long enough they would land on their tails about as often as they would land on their –

Ros Heads. (*He picks up the coin.*)

Guil Which even at first glance does not strike one as a particularly rewarding speculation, in either sense, even without the monkeys. I mean you wouldn't *bet* on it. I mean *I* would, but *you* wouldn't . . . (*As he flips a coin.*)

Ros Heads.

Guil Would you? (*Flips a coin.*)

Ros Heads.

  Repeat.

Heads. (*He looks up at Guil – embarrassed laugh.*) Getting a bit of a bore, isn't it?

Guil (*coldly*) A bore?

Ros Well . . .

Guil What about the suspense?

Ros (*innocently*) What suspense?

  Small pause.

Guil It must be the law of diminishing returns . . . I feel the spell about to be broken. (*Energizing himself somewhat.*)

He takes out a coin, spins it high, catches it, turns it over on to the back of his other hand, studies the coin – and tosses it to Ros. His energy deflates and he sits.

Well, it was an even chance . . . if my calculations are correct.

Ros Eighty-five in a row – beaten the record!

Guil Don't be absurd.

Ros Easily!

Guil (*angry*) Is that *it*, then? Is that all?

Ros What?

Guil A new record? Is that as far as you are prepared to go?

Ros Well . . .

Guil No questions? Not even a pause?

Ros You spun them yourself.

Guil Not a flicker of doubt?

Ros (*aggrieved, aggressive*) Well. I won – didn't I?

Guil (*approaches him – quieter*) And if you'd lost? If they'd come down against you, eighty-five times, one after another, just like that?

Ros (*dumbly*) Eighty-five in a row? *Tails?*

Guil Yes! What would you think?

Ros (*doubtfully*) Well . . . (*jocularly*) Well, I'd have a good look at your coins for a start!

Guil (*retiring*) I'm relieved. At least we can still count on self-interest as a predictable factor . . . I suppose it's the last to go. Your capacity for trust made me wonder if perhaps . . . you, alone . . . (*He turns on him suddenly, reaches out a hand.*) Touch. (*Ros clasps his hand. Guil pulls him up to him. More intensely*) We have been spinning coins together since – (*He releases him almost as violently.*) This is not the first time we have spun coins!

Ros Oh no – we've been spinning coins for as long as I remember.

Guil How long is that?

Ros I forget. Mind you – eighty-five times!

Guil Yes?

Ros It'll take some beating, I imagine.

Guil Is *that* what you imagine? Is that it? No *fear*?

Ros Fear?

Guil (*in fury – flings a coin on the ground*) Fear! The crack that might flood your brain with light!

Ros Heads . . . (*He puts it in his bag.*)

Guil sits despondently. He takes a coin, spins it, lets it fall between his feet. He looks at it, picks it up, throws it to Ros, who puts it in his bag.

Guil takes another coin, spins it, catches it, turns it over on to his other hand, looks at it, and throws it to Ros who puts it in his bag.

Guil takes a third coin, spins it, catches it in his right hand, turns it over on to his left wrist, lobs it in the air, catches it with his left hand, raises his left leg, throws the coin up under it, catches it and turns it over on to the top of his head, where it sits. Ros comes, looks at it, puts it in his bag.

Ros I'm afraid –

Guil So am I.

Ros I'm afraid it isn't your day.

Guil I'm afraid it is.

Small pause.

Ros Eighty-nine.

Guil It must be indicative of something, besides the redistribution of wealth. (*He muses.*) List of possible explanations.

One. I'm willing it. Inside where nothing shows, I am the essence of a man spinning double-headed coins, and betting against himself in private atonement for an unremembered past. (*He spins a coin at Ros.*)

Ros Heads.

Guil Two. Time has stopped dead, and the single experience of one coin being spun once has been repeated ninety times . . . (*He flips a coin, looks at it, tosses it to Ros.*) On the whole, doubtful. Three. Divine intervention, that is to say, a good turn from above concerning him, cf. children of Israel, or retribution from above concerning me, cf. Lot's wife. Four. A spectacular vindication of the principle that each individual coin spun individually (*He spins one*) is as likely to come down heads as tails and therefore should cause no surprise each individual time it does. (*It does. He tosses it to Ros.*)

Ros I've never known anything like it!

Guil And a syllogism: One, he had never known anything like it. Two, he has never known anything to write home about. Three, it is nothing to write home about . . . Home . . . What's the first thing you remember?

Ros Oh, let's see . . . The first thing that comes into my head, you mean?

Guil No – the first thing you remember.

Ros Ah. (*Pause.*) No, it's no good, it's gone. It was a long time ago.

Guil (*patient but edged*) You don't get my meaning. What is the first thing after all the things you've forgotten?

Ros Oh I see. (*Pause.*) I've forgotten the question. (*Guil leaps up and paces.*)

Guil Are you happy?

Ros What?

Guil Content? At ease?

Ros I suppose so.

Guil What are you going to do now?

Ros I don't know. What do you want to do?

Guil I have no desires. None. (*He stops pacing dead.*) There was a messenger . . . that's right. We were sent for. (*He wheels at Ros and raps out –*) Syllogism the second: one, probability is a factor which operates within natural forces. Two, probability is not operating as a factor. Three, we are now within un-, sub- or supernatural forces. Discuss. (*Ros is suitably startled – Acidly*) Not too heatedly.

Ros I'm sorry I – What's the matter with you?

Guil The scientific approach to the examination of phenomena is a defence against the pure emotion of fear. Keep tight hold and continue while there's time. Now – counter to the previous syllogism: tricky one, follow me carefully, it may prove a comfort. If we postulate, and we just have, that within un-, sub- or supernatural forces *the probability is* that the law of probability will not operate as a factor, then we must accept that the probability of the *first* part will not operate as a factor, in which case the law of probability *will* operate as a factor within un-, sub- or supernatural forces. And since it obviously hasn't been doing so, we can take it that we are not held within un-, sub- or supernatural forces after all; in all probability, that is. Which is a great relief to me personally. (*Small pause.*) Which is all very well, except that – (*He continues with tight hysteria, under control.*) We have been spinning coins together since I don't know when, and in all that time (if it *is* all that time) I don't suppose either of us was more than a couple of gold pieces up or down. I hope that doesn't sound surprising because its very unsurprisingness is something I am trying to keep hold of. The equanimity of your average tosser of coins depends upon the law, or rather a tendency, or let us say a probability, or at any rate a mathematically calculable chance, which ensures that he will not upset himself by losing too much nor upset his opponent by winning too often. This made for a kind of harmony and a kind of confidence. It related the fortuitous and the ordained into a reassuring union which we recognized as nature. The sun came up about as often as it went down, in the long run, and a coin showed heads about as often as it showed tails. Then a messenger arrived. We had been sent for. Nothing else happened. Ninety-two coins spun consecutively have come down heads ninety-two consecutive times . . . and for the last three minutes on the wind of a windless day I have heard the sound of drums and flute . . .

Ros (*cutting his fingernails*) Another curious scientific phenomenon is the fact that the fingernails grow after death, as does the beard.

Guil What?

Ros (*loud*) Beard!

Guil But you're not dead.

Ros (*irritated*) I didn't say they *started* to grow after death! (*Pause, calmer.*) The fingernails also grow before birth, though *not* the beard.

Guil *What?*

Ros (*shouts*) Beard! What's the matter with you? (*reflectively*) The toenails, on the other hand, never grow at all.

Guil (*bemused*) The toenails on the other hand never grow at all?

Ros Do they? It's a funny thing – I cut my fingernails all the time, and every time I think to cut them, they need cutting. Now, for instance. And yet, I never, to the best of my knowledge, cut my toenails. They ought to be curled under my feet by now, but it doesn't happen. I never think about them. Perhaps I cut them absent-mindedly, when I'm thinking of something else.

Guil (*tensed up by this rambling*) Do you remember the first thing that happened today?

Ros (*promptly*) I woke up, I suppose. (*Triggered.*) Oh – I've got it now – that man, a foreigner, he woke us up –

Guil A messenger. (*He relaxes, sits.*)

Ros That's it – pale sky before dawn, a man standing on his saddle to bang on the shutters – shouts – What's all the row about?! Clear off! – But then he called our names. You remember that – this man woke us up.

Guil Yes.

Ros We were sent for.

Guil Yes.

Ros That's why we're here. (*He looks round, seems doubtful, then the explanation.*) Travelling.

Guil Yes.

Ros (*dramatically*) It was urgent – a matter of extreme urgency, a royal summons, his very words: official business and no questions asked – lights in the stableyard, saddle up and off headlong and hotfoot across the land, our guides outstripped in breakneck pursuit of our duty! Fearful lest we come too late!! (*Small pause.*)

Guil Too late for what?

Ros How do I know? We haven't got there yet.

Guil Then what are we doing here, I ask myself.

Ros You might well ask.

Guil We better get on.

Ros You might well think.

Guil We better get on.

Ros (*actively*) Right! (*Pause.*) On where?

Guil Forward.

Ros (*forward to footlights*) Ah. (*Hesitates.*) Which way do we – (*He turns round.*) Which way did we – ?

Guil Practically starting from scratch . . . An awakening, a man standing on his saddle to bang on the shutters, our names shouted in a certain dawn, a message, a summons . . . A new record for heads and tails. We have not been . . . picked out . . . simply to be abandoned . . . set loose to find our own way . . . We are entitled to some direction . . . I would have thought.

Ros (*alert, listening*) I say – ! I say –

Guil Yes?

Ros I can hear – I thought I heard – music.

Guil raises himself.

Guil Yes?

Ros Like a band. (*He looks around, laughs embarrassedly, expiating himself.*) It sounded like – a band. Drums.

Guil Yes.

Ros (*relaxes*) It couldn't have been real.

Guil 'The colours red, blue and green are real. The colour yellow is a mystical experience shared by everybody' – demolish.

Ros (*at edge of stage*) It must have been thunder. Like drums . . .

By the end of the next speech, the band is faintly audible.

Guil A man breaking his journey between one place and another at a third place of no name, character, population or significance, sees a unicorn cross his path and disappear. That in itself is startling, but there are precedents for mystical encounters of various kinds or, to be less extreme, a choice of persuasions to put it down to fancy; until – 'My God,' says a second man, 'I must be dreaming, I thought I saw a unicorn.' At which point, a dimension is added that makes the experience as alarming as it will ever be. A third witness, you understand, adds no further dimension but only spreads it thinner, and a fourth thinner still, and the more witnesses there are the thinner it gets and the more reasonable it becomes until it is as thin

as reality, the name we give to the common experience . . .
'Look, look!' recites the crowd. 'A horse with an arrow in
its forehead! It must have been mistaken for a deer.'

Ros (*eagerly*) I knew all along it was a band.

Guil (*tiredly*) He knew all along it was a band.

Ros Here they come!

Guil (*at the last moment before they enter – wistfully*) I'm
sorry it wasn't a unicorn. It would have been nice to have
unicorns.

*The Tragedians are six in number, including a small boy
(Alfred). Two pull and push a cart piled with props and
belongings. There is also a Drummer, a Horn-Player
and a Flautist. The Spokesman ('the Player') has no
instrument. He brings up the rear and is the first to
notice them.*

Player Halt!

The Group turns and halts.

(*joyously*) An audience!

Ros and Guil half rise.

Don't move!

They sink back. He regards them fondly.

Perfect! A lucky thing we came along.

Ros For us?

Player Let us hope so. But to meet two gentlemen on the
road – we would not hope to meet them off it.

Ros No?

Player Well met, in fact, and just in time.

Ros Why's that?

Player Why, we grow rusty and you catch us at the very point of decadence – by this time tomorrow we might have forgotten everything we ever knew. That's a thought, isn't it? (*He laughs generously.*) We'd be back where we started – improvising.

Ros Tumblers, are you?

Player We can give you a tumble if that's your taste, and times being what they are . . . Otherwise, for a jingle of coin we can do you a selection of gory romances, full of fine cadence and corpses, pirated from the Italian; and it doesn't take much to make a jingle – even a single coin has music in it.

They all flourish and bow, raggedly.

Tragedians, at your command.

Ros and Guil have got to their feet.

Ros My name is Guildenstern, and this is Rosencrantz. (*Guil confers briefly with him.*)

(*without embarrassment*) I'm sorry – *his* name's Guildenstern, and *I'm* Rosencrantz.

Player A pleasure. We've played to bigger, of course, but quality counts for something. I recognized you at once –

Ros And who are we?

Player – as fellow artists.

Ros I thought we were gentlemen.

Player For some of us it is performance, for others, patronage. They are two sides of the same coin, or, let us say, being as there are so many of us, the same side of two coins. (*Bows again.*) Don't clap too loudly – it's a very old world.

Ros What is your line?

Player Tragedy, sir. Deaths and disclosures, universal and particular, dénouements both unexpected and inexorable, transvestite melodrama on all levels including the suggestive. We transport you into a world of intrigue and illusion . . . clowns, if you like, murderers – we can do you ghosts and battles, on the skirmish level, heroes, villains, tormented lovers – set pieces in the poetic vein; we can do you rapiers or rape or both, by all means, faithless wives and ravished virgins – flagrante delicto at a price, but that comes under realism for which there are special terms. Getting warm, am I?

Ros (*doubtfully*) Well, I don't know . . .

Player It costs little to watch, and little more if you happen to get caught up in the action, if that's your taste and times being what they are.

Ros What are they?

Player Indifferent.

Ros Bad?

Player Wicked. Now what precisely is your pleasure? (*He turns to the Tragedians.*) Gentlemen, disport yourselves. (*The Tragedians shuffle into some kind of line.*) There! See anything you like?

Ros (*doubtful, innocent*) What do they do?

Player Let your imagination run riot. They are beyond surprise.

Ros And how much?

Player To take part?

Ros To watch.

Player Watch what?

Ros A private performance.

Player How private?

Ros Well, there are only two of us. Is that enough?

Player For an audience, disappointing. For voyeurs, about average.

Ros What's the difference?

Player Ten guilders.

Ros (*horrified*) Ten *guilders*!

Player I mean eight.

Ros Together?

Player Each. I don't think you understand –

Ros What are you *saying*?

Player What am I saying – seven.

Ros Where have you *been*?

Player Roundabout. A nest of children carries the custom of the town. Juvenile companies, they are the fashion. But they cannot match our repertoire . . . we'll stoop to anything if that's your bent . . .

He regards Ros meaningfully but Ros returns the stare blankly.

Ros They'll grow up.

Player (*giving up*) There's one born every minute. (*to Tragedians*) On-ward!

The Tragedians start to resume their burdens and their journey. Guil stirs himself at last.

Guil Where are you going?

Player Ha-alt!

They halt and turn.

Home, sir.

Guil Where from?

Player Home. We're travelling people. We take our chances where we find them.

Guil It was chance, then?

Player Chance?

Guil You found us.

Player Oh yes.

Guil You were looking?

Player Oh no.

Guil Chance, then.

Player Or fate.

Guil Yours or ours?

Player It could hardly be one without the other.

Guil Fate, then.

Player Oh yes. We have no control. Tonight we play to the court. Or the night after. Or to the tavern. Or not.

Guil Perhaps I can use my influence.

Player At the tavern?

Guil At the court. I would say I have some influence.

Player Would you say so?

Guil I have influence yet.

Player Yet what?

Guil seizes the Player violently.

Guil I have influence!

The Player does not resist. Guil loosens his hold. More calmly.

You said something – about getting caught up in the action –

Player (*gaily freeing himself*) I did! – I did! – You're quicker than your friend . . . (*confidingly*) Now for a handful of guilders I happen to have a private and uncut performance of the Rape of the Sabine Women – or rather woman, or rather Alfred – (*over his shoulder*) Get your skirt on, Alfred –

The Boy starts struggling into a female robe.

. . . and for eight you can participate.

Guil backs, Player follows.

. . . taking either part.

Guil backs.

. . . or both for ten.

Guil tries to turn away. Player holds his sleeve.

. . . with encores –

Guil smashes the Player across the face. The Player recoils. Guil stands trembling.

(*resigned and quiet*) Get your skirt off, Alfred . . .

Alfred struggles out of his half-on robe.

Guil (*shaking with rage and fright*) It could have been – it didn't have to be *obscene* . . . It could have been – a bird

out of season, dropping bright-feathered on my shoulder
. . . It could have been a tongueless dwarf standing by the
road to point the way . . . I was *prepared*. But it's this, is
it? No enigma, no dignity, nothing classical, portentous,
only this – a comic pornographer and a rabble of
prostitutes . . .

Player (*acknowledging the description with a sweep of his
hat, bowing: sadly*) You should have caught us in better
times. We were purists then. (*Straightens up.*) On-ward.

The Players make to leave.

Ros (*his voice has changed: he has caught on*) Excuse me!

Player Ha-alt!

They halt.

A-al-l-fred!

Alfred resumes the struggle. The Player comes forward.

Ros You're not – ah – exclusively players, then?

Player We're inclusively players, sir.

Ros So you give – exhibitions?

Player Performances, sir.

Ros Yes, of course. There's more money in that, is there?

Player There's more trade, sir.

Ros Times being what they are.

Player Yes.

Ros Indifferent.

Player Completely.

Ros You know I'd no idea –

Player No.

Ros I mean, I've *heard* of – but I've never actually –

Player No.

Ros I mean, what exactly do you *do*?

Player We keep to our usual stuff, more or less, only inside out. We do on stage the things that are supposed to happen off. Which is a kind of integrity, if you look on every exit being an entrance somewhere else.

Ros (*nervy, loud*) Well, I'm not really the type of man who – no, but don't hurry off – sit down and tell us about some of the things people ask you to do – (*The Player turns away.*)

Player On-ward!

Ros Just a minute!

They turn and look at him without expression.

Well, all right – I wouldn't mind seeing – just an idea of the kind of – (*bravely*) What will you do for that? (*And tosses a single coin on the ground between them. The Player spits at the coin, from where he stands. The Tragedians demur, trying to get at the coin. He kicks and cuffs them back.*)

Player On!

Alfred is still half in and out of his robe. The Player cuffs him. To Alfred.

What are you playing at?

Ros is shamed into fury.

Ros Filth! Disgusting – I'll report you to the authorities – *perverts*! I know your game all right, it's all filth!

The Players are about to leave. Guil has remained detached.

Guil (*casually*) Do you like a bet?

The Tragedians turn and look interested. The Player comes forward.

Player What kind of bet did you have in mind?

Guil walks half the distance towards the Player, stops with his foot over the coin.

Guil Double or quits.

Player Well . . . heads.

Guil raises his foot. The Player bends. The Tragedians crowd round. Relief and congratulations. The Player picks up the coin. Guil throws him a second coin.

Guil Again?

Some of the Tragedians are for it, others against.

Evens.

The Player nods and tosses the coin.

Heads.

It is. He picks it up.

Again.

Guil spins coin.

Player Heads.

It is. The Player picks up coin. He has two coins again. He spins one.

Guil Heads.

It is. Guil picks it up. Then tosses it immediately.

Player (*fractional hesitation*) Tails.

> *But it's heads. Guil picks it up. The Player tosses down his last coin by way of paying up, and turns away. Guil doesn't pick it up; he puts his foot on it.*

Guil Heads.

Player No!

> *Pause. The Tragedians are against this. Apologetically.*

They don't like the odds.

Guil (*lifts his foot, squats; picks up the coin still squatting; looks up*) You were right – heads. (*Spins it, slaps his hand on it, on the floor.*) Heads I win.

Player No.

Guil (*uncovers coin*) Right again. (*Repeat.*) Heads I win.

Player No.

Guil (*uncovers coin*) And right again. (*Repeat.*) Heads I win.

Player *No!*

> *He turns away, the Tragedians with him. Guil stands up, comes close.*

Guil Would you believe it? (*Stands back, relaxes, smiles.*) Bet me the year of my birth doubled is an odd number.

Player *Your* birth –!

Guil If you don't trust me don't bet with me.

Player Would you trust *me*?

Guil *Bet* me then.

Player My birth?

Guil Odd numbers you win.

Player You're on –

The Tragedians have come forward, wide awake.

Guil Good. Year of your birth. Double it. Even numbers I win, odd numbers I lose.

Silence. An awful sigh as the Tragedians realize that any number doubled is even. Then a terrible row as they object. Then a terrible silence.

Player We have no money.

Guil turns to him.

Guil Ah. Then what *have* you got?

The Player silently brings Alfred forward. Guil regards Alfred sadly.

Was it for this?

Player It is the best we've got.

Guil (*looking up and around*) Then the times are bad indeed.

The Player starts to speak, protestation, but Guil turns on him viciously.

The very *air* stinks.

The Player moves back. Guil moves down to the footlights and turns.

Come here, Alfred.

Alfred moves down and stands, frightened and small. Gently.

Do you lose often?

Alfred Yes, sir.

Guil Then what could you have left to lose?

Alfred Nothing, sir.

Pause. Guil regards him.

Guil Do you like being . . . an actor?

Alfred No, sir.

Guil looks around, at the audience.

Guil You and I, Alfred – we could create a dramatic precedent here.

And Alfred, who has been near to tears, starts to sniffle.

Come, come, Alfred, this is no way to fill the theatres of Europe.

The Player has moved down, to remonstrate with Alfred. Guil cuts him off again. Viciously.

Do you know any good plays?

Player Plays?

Ros (*coming forward, faltering shyly*) Exhibitions . . .

Guil I thought you said you were actors.

Player (*dawning*) Oh. Oh well, we *are*. We are. But there hasn't been much call –

Guil You lost. Well then – one of the Greeks, perhaps? You're familiar with the tragedies of antiquity, are you? The great homicidal classics? Matri, patri, fratri, sorori, uxori and it goes without saying –

Ros Saucy –

Guil – Suicidal – hm? Maidens aspiring to godheads –

Ros And vice versa –

23

Guil Your kind of thing, is it?

Player Well, no, I can't say it is, really. We're more of the blood, love and rhetoric school.

Guil Well, I'll leave the choice to you, if there is anything to choose between them.

Player They're hardly divisible, sir – well, I can do you blood and love without the rhetoric, and I can do you blood and rhetoric without the love, and I can do you all three concurrent or consecutive, but I can't do you love and rhetoric without the blood. Blood is compulsory – they're all blood, you see.

Guil Is that what people want?

Player It's what we do.

Small pause. He turns away. Guil touches Alfred on the shoulder.

Guil (*wry, gentle*) Thank you; we'll let you know.

The Player has moved upstage. Alfred follows.

Player (*to Tragedians*) Thirty-eight!

Ros (*moving across, fascinated and hopeful*) Position?

Player Sir?

Ros One of your – tableaux?

Player No, sir.

Ros Oh.

Player (*to the Tragedians, now departing with their cart, already taking various props off it*) Entrances there and there (*Indicating upstage*).

The Player has not moved his position for his last four lines. He does not move now. Guil waits.

Guil Well . . . aren't you going to change into your costume?

Player I never change out of it, sir.

Guil Always in character.

Player That's it.

Pause.

Guil Aren't you going to – come *on*?

Player I *am* on.

Guil But if you *are* on, you can't *come* on. *Can* you?

Player I *start* on.

Guil But it hasn't *started*. Go on. We'll look out for you.

Player I'll give you a wave.

He does not move. His immobility is now pointed, and getting awkward. Pause. Ros walks up to him till they are face to face.

Ros Excuse me.

Pause. The Player lifts his downstage foot. It was covering Guil's coin. Ros puts his foot on the coin. Smiles.

Thank you.

The Player turns and goes. Ros has bent for the coin.

Guil (*moving out*) Come on.

Ros I say – that was lucky.

Guil (*turning*) What?

Ros It was tails.

He tosses the coin to Guil who catches it.

*Simultaneously – a lighting change sufficient to alter the
exterior mood into interior, but nothing violent. And
Ophelia runs on in some alarm, holding up her skirts –
followed by **Hamlet**.*

*Ophelia has been sewing and she holds the garment.
They are both mute. Hamlet, with his doublet all
unbraced, no hat upon his head, his stockings fouled,
ungartered and down-gyved to his ankle, pale as his
shirt, his knees knocking each other . . . and with a look
so piteous, he takes her by the wrist and holds her hard,
then he goes to the length of his arm, and with his other
hand over his brow, falls to such perusal of her face as
he would draw it . . . At last, with a little shaking of his
arm, and thrice his head waving up and down, he raises
a sigh so piteous and profound that it does seem to
shatter all his bulk and end his being. That done he lets
her go, and with his head over his shoulder turned, he
goes out backwards without taking his eyes off her . . .
she runs off in the opposite direction.*

*Ros and Guil have frozen. Guil unfreezes first. He
jumps at Ros.*

Guil Come on!

But a flourish – enter Claudius and Gertrude, attended.

Claudius Welcome, dear Rosencrantz . . . (*He raises a
hand at Guil while Ros bows – Guil bows late and
hurriedly*) . . . and Guildenstern.

*He raises a hand at Ros while Guil bows to him – Ros is
still straightening up from his previous bow and half
way up he bows down again. With his head down, he
twists to look at Guil, who is on the way up.*

Moreover that we did much long to see you,
the need we have to use you did provoke
our hasty sending.

Ros and Guil still adjusting their clothing for Claudius's presence.

Something have you heard
Of Hamlet's transformation, so call it,
Sith nor th'exterior nor the inward man
Resembles that it was. What it should be,
More than his father's death, that thus hath put him,
So much from th'understanding of himself,
I cannot dream of. I entreat you both
That, being of so young days brought up with him
And sith so neighboured to his youth and haviour
That you vouchsafe your rest here in our court
Some little time, so by your companies
To draw him on to pleasures, and to gather
So much as from occasion you may glean,
Whether aught to us unknown afflicts him thus,
That opened lies within our remedy.

Gertrude Good (*fractional suspense*) gentlemen . . . (*They both bow.*)

He hath much talked of you,
And sure I am, two men there is not living
To whom he more adheres. If it will please you
To show us so much gentry and goodwill
As to expand your time with us awhile
For the supply and profit of our hope,
Your visitation shall receive such thanks
As fits a king's remembrance.

Ros Both your majesties
Might, by the sovereign power you have of us,
Put your dread pleasures more into command
Than to entreaty.

Guil We both obey,
And here give up ourselves in the full bent

To lay our service freely at your feet,
To be commanded.

Claudius Thanks, Rosencrantz (*Turning to Ros who is caught unprepared, while Guil bows.*) and gentle Guildenstern (*Turning to Guil who is bent double*).

Gertrude (*correcting*) Thanks, Guildenstern (*Turning to Ros, who bows as Guil checks upward movements to bow too – both bent double, squinting at each other.*) . . . and gentle Rosencrantz. (*Turning to Guil, both straightening up – Guil checks again and bows again.*)

And I beseech you instantly to visit
My too much changed son. Go, some of you,
And bring these gentlemen where Hamlet is.

> *Two Attendants exit backwards, indicating that Ros and Guil should follow.*

Guil Heaven make our presence and our practices
Pleasant and helpful to him.

Gertrude Ay, amen!

> *Ros and Guil move towards a downstage wing. Before they get there, Polonius enters. They stop and bow to him. He nods and hurries upstage to Claudius. They turn to look at him.*

Polonius The ambassadors from Norway, my good lord, are joyfully returned.

Claudius Thou still hast been the father of good news.

Polonius Have I, my lord? Assure you, my good liege,
I hold to my duty as I hold my soul,
Both to my God and to my gracious King;
And I do think, or else this brain of mine
Hunts not the trail of policy so sure

As it hath used to do, that I have found
The very cause of Hamlet's lunacy . . .

   Exeunt – leaving Ros and Guil.

Ros I want to go home.

Guil Don't let them confuse you.

Ros I'm out of my step here –

Guil We'll soon be home and high – dry and home – I'll –

Ros It's all over my *depth* –

Guil I'll hie you home and –

Ros – out of my head –

Guil – dry you high and –

Ros (*cracking, high*) – over my step over my head body! –
I tell you it's all stopping to a death, it's boding to a depth,
stepping to a head, it's all heading to a dead stop –

Guil (*the nursemaid*) There! . . . and we'll soon be home
and dry . . . and *high* and dry . . . (*rapidly*) Has it ever
happened to you that all of a sudden and for no reason at
all you haven't the faintest idea how to spell the word –
'wife' – or 'house' – because when you write it down you
just can't remember ever having seen those letters in that
order before . . . ?

Ros I remember –

Guil Yes?

Ros I remember when there were no questions.

Guil There were always questions. To exchange one set
for another is no great matter.

Ros Answers, yes. There were answers to everything.

Guil You've forgotten.

Ros (*flaring*) I haven't forgotten – how I used to remember my own name – and yours, oh *yes!* There were answers everywhere you *looked*. There was no question about it – people knew who I was and if they didn't they asked and I told them.

Guil You did, the trouble is, each of them is . . . plausible, without being instinctive. All your life you live so close to truth, it becomes a permanent blur in the corner of your eye, and when something nudges it into outline it is like being ambushed by a grotesque. A man standing in his saddle in the half-lit half-alive dawn banged on the shutters and called two names. He was just a hat and a cloak levitating in the grey plume of his own breath, but when he called we came. That much is certain – we came.

Ros Well I can tell you I'm sick to death of it. I don't care one way or another, so why don't you make up your mind.

Guil We can't afford anything quite so arbitrary. Nor did we come all this way for a christening. All *that* – preceded us. But we are comparatively fortunate; we might have been left to sift the whole field of human nomenclature, like two blind men looting a bazaar for their own portraits . . . At least we are presented with alternatives.

Ros Well as from now –

Guil – But not choice.

Ros You made me look ridiculous in there.

Guil I looked just as ridiculous as you did.

Ros (*an anguished cry*) Consistency is all I ask!

Guil (*low, wry rhetoric*) Give us this day our daily mask.

Ros (*a dying fall*) I want to go home. (*Moves.*) Which way did we come in? I've lost my sense of direction.

Guil The only beginning is birth and the only end is death – if you can't count on that, what can you count on?

They connect again.

Ros We don't owe anything to anyone.

Guil We've been caught up. Your smallest action sets off another somewhere else, and is set off by it. Keep an eye open, an ear cocked. Tread warily, follow instructions. We'll be all right.

Ros For how long?

Guil Till events have played themselves out. There's a logic at work – it's all done for you, don't worry. Enjoy it. Relax. To be taken in hand and led, like being a child again, even without the innocence, a child – It's like being given a prize, an extra slice of childhood when you least expect it, as a prize for being good, or compensation for never having had one . . . Do I contradict myself?

Ros I can't remember . . . What have we got to go on?

Guil We have been briefed. Hamlet's transformation. What do you recollect?

Ros Well, he's changed, hasn't he? The exterior and inward man fails to resemble –

Guil Draw him on to pleasures – glean what afflicts him.

Ros Something more than his father's death –

Guil He's always talking about us – there aren't two people living whom he dotes on more than us.

Ros We cheer him up – find out what's the matter –

Guil Exactly, it's a matter of asking the right questions and giving away as little as we can. It's a game.

Ros And then we can go?

Guil And receive such thanks as fits a king's remembrance.

Ros I like the sound of that. What do you think he means by remembrance?

Guil He doesn't forget his friends.

Ros Would you care to estimate?

Guil Difficult to say, really – some kings tend to be amnesiac, others I suppose – the opposite, whatever that is . . .

Ros Yes – but –

Guil Elephantine . . . ?

Ros Not how long – how much?

Guil *Retentive* – he's a very retentive king, a royal retainer . . .

Ros What are you playing at?

Guil Words, words. They're all we have to go on.

  Pause.

Ros Shouldn't we be doing something – constructive?

Guil What did you have in mind? . . . A short, blunt human pyramid . . . ?

Ros We could go.

Guil Where?

Ros After him.

Guil Why? They've got us placed now – if we start moving around, we'll all be chasing each other all night.

Hiatus.

Ros (*at footlights*) How very intriguing! (*Turns.*) I feel like a spectator – an appalling prospect. The only thing that makes it bearable is the irrational belief that somebody interesting will come on in a minute . . .

Guil See anyone?

Ros No. You?

Guil No. (*At footlights*) What a fine persecution – to be kept intrigued without ever quite being enlightened . . . (*Pause.*) We've had no practice.

Ros We could play at questions.

Guil What good would that do?

Ros Practice!

Guil Statement! One-love.

Ros Cheating!

Guil How?

Ros I hadn't started yet.

Guil Statement. Two-love.

Ros Are you counting that?

Guil What?

Ros Are you counting that?

Guil Foul! No repetitions. Three-love. First game to . . .

Ros I'm not going to play if you're going to be like that.

Guil Whose serve?

Ros Hah?

Guil Foul! No grunts. Love-one.

Ros Whose go?

Guil Why?

Ros Why not?

Guil What for?

Ros Foul! No synonyms! One-all.

Guil What in God's name is going on?

Ros Foul! No rhetoric. Two-one.

Guil What does it all add up to?

Ros Can't you guess?

Guil Were you addressing me?

Ros Is there anyone else?

Guil Who?

Ros How would I know?

Guil Why do you ask?

Ros Are you serious?

Guil Was that rhetoric?

Ros No.

Guil Statement! Two-all. Game point.

Ros What's the matter with you today?

Guil When?

Ros What?

Guil Are you deaf?

Ros Am I dead?

Guil Yes or no?

Ros Is there a choice?

Guil Is there a God?

Ros Foul! No *non sequiturs*, three-two, one game all.

Guil (*seriously*) What's your name?

Ros What's yours?

Guil I asked first.

Ros Statement. One-love.

Guil What's your name when you're at home?

Ros What's yours?

Guil When I'm at home?

Ros Is it different at home?

Guil What home?

Ros Haven't you got one?

Guil Why do you ask?

Ros What are you driving at?

Guil (*with emphasis*) What's your name?!

Ros Repetition. Two-love. Match point to me.

Guil (*seizing him violently*) WHO DO YOU THINK YOU ARE?

Ros Rhetoric! Game and match! (*Pause.*) Where's it going to end?

Guil That's the question.

Ros It's *all* questions.

Guil Do you think it matters?

Ros Doesn't it matter to you?

Guil Why should it matter?

Ros What does it matter why?

Guil (*teasing gently*) Doesn't it *matter* why it matters?

Ros (*rounding on him*) What's the *matter* with you?

Pause.

Guil It doesn't matter.

Ros (*voice in the wilderness*) . . . What's the game?

Guil What are the rules?

*Enter Hamlet behind, crossing the stage, reading a book
– as he is about to disappear Guil notices him.*

Guil (*sharply*) Rosencrantz!

Ros (*jumps*) What!

Hamlet goes. Triumph dawns on them, they smile.

Guil There! How was that?

Ros Clever!

Guil Natural?

Ros Instinctive.

Guil Got it in your head?

Ros I take my hat off to you.

Guil Shake hands.

They do.

Ros Now I'll try you – Guil –!

Guil – Not yet – catch me unawares.

Ros Right. (*They separate. Pause. Aside to Guil*) Ready?

Guil (*explodes*) Don't be stupid.

Ros Sorry.

   Pause.

Guil (*snaps*) Guildenstern!

Ros (*jumps*) What? (*He is immediately crestfallen, Guil is disgusted.*)

Guil Consistency is all I ask!

Ros (*quietly*) Immortality is all I seek . . .

Guil (*dying fall*) Give us this day our daily week . . .

   Beat.

Ros Who was that?

Guil Didn't you know him?

Ros He didn't know me.

Guil He didn't see you.

Ros I didn't see him.

Guil We shall see. I *hardly* knew him, he's changed.

Ros You could see that?

Guil Transformed.

Ros How do you know?

Guil Inside and out.

Ros I see.

Guil He's not himself.

Ros He's changed.

Guil I could see that. (*Beat.*) Glean what afflicts him.

Ros Me?

Guil Him.

Ros How?

Guil Question and answer. Old ways are the best ways.

Ros He's afflicted.

Guil You question, I'll answer.

Ros He's not himself, you know.

Guil I'm him, you see.

   Beat.

Ros Who am I then?

Guil You're yourself.

Ros And he's you?

Guil Not a bit of it.

Ros Are you afflicted?

Guil That's the idea. Are you ready?

Ros Let's go back a bit.

Guil I'm afflicted.

Ros I see.

Guil Glean what afflicts me.

Ros Right.

Guil Question and answer.

Ros How should I begin?

Guil Address me.

Ros My dear Guildenstern!

Guil (*quietly*) You've forgotten – haven't you?

Ros My dear Rosencrantz!

Guil (*great control*) I don't think you quite understand. What we are attempting is a hypothesis in which *I* answer for *him*, while *you* ask me questions.

Ros Ah! Ready?

Guil You know what to do?

Ros What?

Guil Are you stupid?

Ros Pardon?

Guil Are you deaf?

Ros Did you speak?

Guil (*admonishing*) Not now –

Ros Statement.

Guil (*shouts*) Not now! (*Pause.*) If I had any doubts, or rather hopes, they are dispelled. What could we possibly have in common except our situation? (*They separate and sit.*) Perhaps he'll come back this way.

Ros Should we go?

Guil Why?

   Pause.

Ros (*starts up. Snaps fingers*) Oh! You mean – you pretend to be *him*, and *I* ask you questions!

Guil (*dry*) Very good.

Ros You had me confused.

Guil I could see I had.

Ros How should I begin?

Guil Address me.

They stand and face each other, posing.

Ros My honoured Lord!

Guil My dear Rosencrantz!

Pause.

Ros Am I pretending to be you, then?

Guil Certainly not. If you like. Shall we continue?

Ros Question and answer.

Guil Right.

Ros Right. My honoured lord!

Guil My dear fellow!

Ros How are you?

Guil Afflicted!

Ros Really? In what way?

Guil Transformed.

Ros Inside or out?

Guil Both.

Ros I see. (*Pause.*) Not much new there.

Guil Go into details. *Delve.* Probe the background, establish the situation.

Ros So – so your uncle is the king of Denmark?!

Guil And my father before him.

Ros His father before him?

Guil No, my father before him.

Ros But surely –

Guil You might well ask.

Ros Let me get it straight. Your father was king. You were his only son. Your father dies. You are of age. Your uncle becomes king.

Guil Yes.

Ros Unorthodox.

Guil Undid me.

Ros Undeniable. Where were you?

Guil In Germany.

Ros Usurpation, then.

Guil He slipped in.

Ros Which reminds me.

Guil Well, it would.

Ros I don't want to be personal.

Guil It's common knowledge.

Ros Your mother's marriage.

Guil He slipped in.

   Beat.

Ros (*lugubriously*) His body was still warm.

Guil So was hers.

Ros Extraordinary.

Guil Indecent.

Ros Hasty.

Guil Suspicious.

Ros It makes you think.

Guil Don't think I haven't thought of it.

Ros And with her husband's brother.

Guil They were close.

Ros She went to him –

Guil – Too close –

Ros – for comfort.

Guil It looks bad.

Ros It adds up.

Guil Incest to adultery.

Ros Would you go so far?

Guil Never.

Ros To sum up: your father, whom you love, dies, you are his heir, you come back to find that hardly was the corpse cold before his young brother popped on to his throne and into his sheets, thereby offending both legal and natural practice. Now why exactly are you behaving in this extraordinary manner?

Guil I can't imagine! (*Pause.*) But all that is well known, common property. Yet he sent for us. And we did come.

Ros (*alert, ear cocked*) I say! I heard music –

Guil We're here.

Ros – Like a band – I thought I heard a band.

Guil Rosencrantz . . .

Ros (*absently, still listening*) What?

  Pause, short.

Guil (*gently wry*) Guildenstern . . .

Ros (*irritated by the repetition*) What?

Guil Don't you discriminate at all?

Ros (*turning dumbly*) Wha'?

  Pause.

Guil Go and see if he's there.

Ros Who?

Guil There.

  *Ros goes to an upstage wing, looks, returns, formally
  making his report.*

Ros Yes.

Guil What is he doing?

  Ros repeats movement.

Ros Talking.

Guil To himself?

  Ros starts to move. Guil cuts in impatiently.

Is he alone?

Ros No.

Guil Then he's not talking to himself, is he?

Ros Not *by* himself . . . Coming this way, I think.
(*shiftily*) Should we go?

Guil Why? We're marked now.

Hamlet enters, backwards, talking, followed by Polonius, upstage. Ros and Guil occupy the two downstage corners looking upstage.

Hamlet . . . for you yourself, sir, should be as old as I am if like a crab you could go backward.

Polonius (*aside*) Though this be madness, yet there is method in it. Will you walk out of the air, my lord?

Hamlet Into my grave.

Polonius Indeed, that's out of the air.

Hamlet crosses to upstage exit, Polonius asiding unintelligibly until –

My lord, I will take my leave of you.

Hamlet You cannot take from me anything that I will more willingly part withal – except my life, except my life, except my life . . .

Polonius (*crossing downstage*) Fare you well, my lord. (*to Ros*) You go to seek Lord Hamlet? There he is.

Ros (*to Polonius*) God save you sir.

Polonius goes.

Guil (*calls upstage to Hamlet*) My honoured lord!

Ros My most dear lord!

Hamlet centred upstage, turns to them.

Hamlet My excellent good friends! How dost thou Guildenstern?

Coming downstage with an arm raised to Ros, Guil meanwhile bowing to no greeting. Hamlet corrects himself. Still to Ros.

Ah Rosencrantz!

They laugh good-naturedly at the mistake. They all meet midstage, turn upstage to walk, Hamlet in the middle, arm over each shoulder.

Hamlet Good lads, how do you both?

Blackout.

Act Two

Hamlet, Ros and Guil talking, the continuation of the previous scene. Their conversation, on the move, is indecipherable at first. The first intelligible line is Hamlet's, coming at the end of a short speech – see Shakespeare Act II, scene ii.

Hamlet S'blood, there is something in this more than natural, if philosophy could find it out.

A flourish from the Tragedians' band.

Guil There are the players.

Hamlet Gentlemen, you are welcome to Elsinore. Your hands, come then. (*He takes their hands.*) The appurtenance of welcome is fashion and ceremony. Let me comply with you in this garb, lest my extent to the players (which I tell you must show fairly outwards) should more appear like entertainment than yours. You are welcome. (*about to leave*) But my uncle-father and aunt-mother are deceived.

Guil In what, my dear lord?

Hamlet I am but mad north north-west; when the wind is southerly I know a hawk from a handsaw.

Polonius enters as Guil turns away.

Polonius Well be with you gentlemen.

Hamlet (*to Ros*) Mark you, Guildenstern (*uncertainly to Guil*) and you too; at each ear a hearer. That great baby you see there is not yet out of his swaddling clouts . . .

He takes Ros upstage with him, talking together.

Polonius My Lord! I have news to tell you.

Hamlet (*releasing Ros and mimicking*) My lord, I have news to tell you . . . When Roscius was an actor in Rome . . .

Ros comes downstage to re-join Guil.

Polonius (*as he follows Hamlet out*) The actors are come hither my lord.

Hamlet Buzz, buzz.

Exeunt Hamlet and Polonius.
Ros and Guil ponder. Each reluctant to speak first.

Guil Hm?

Ros Yes?

Guil What?

Ros I thought you . . .

Guil No.

Ros Ah.

Pause.

Guil I think we can say we made some headway.

Ros You think so?

Guil I think we can say that.

Ros I think we can say he made us look ridiculous.

Guil We played it close to the chest of course.

Ros (*derisively*) 'Question and answer. Old ways are the best ways'! He was scoring off us all down the line.

Guil He caught us on the wrong foot once or twice, perhaps, but I thought we gained some ground.

Ros (*simply*) He murdered us.

Guil He might have had the edge.

Ros (*roused*) Twenty-seven-three, and you think he might have had the edge?! He *murdered* us.

Guil What about our evasions?

Ros Oh, our evasions were lovely. 'Were you sent for?' he says. 'My lord, we were sent for . . .' I didn't know where to put myself.

Guil He had six rhetoricals -

Ros It was question and answer, all right. Twenty-seven questions he got out in ten minutes, and answered three. I was waiting for you to *delve*. 'When is he going to start *delving*?' I asked myself.

Guil – And two repetitions.

Ros Hardly a leading question between us.

Guil We got his *symptoms*, didn't we?

Ros Half of what he said meant something else, and the other half didn't mean anything at all.

Guil Thwarted ambition – a sense of grievance, that's my diagnosis.

Ros Six rhetorical and two repetition, leaving nineteen of which we answered fifteen. And what did we get in return? He's depressed! . . . Denmark's a prison and he'd rather live in a nutshell; some shadow-play about the nature of ambition, which never got down to cases, and finally one direct question which might have led somewhere, and led in fact to his illuminating claim to tell a hawk from a handsaw.

Pause.

Guil When the wind is southerly.

Ros And the weather's clear.

Guil And when it isn't he can't.

Ros He's at the mercy of the elements. (*Licks his finger and holds it up – facing audience.*) Is that southerly? (*They stare at audience.*)

Guil It doesn't *look* southerly. What made you think so?

Ros I didn't *say* I think so. It could be northerly for all I know.

Guil I wouldn't have thought so.

Ros Well, if you're going to be dogmatic.

Guil Wait a minute – we came from roughly south according to a rough map.

Ros I see. Well, which way did we come in? (*Guil looks round vaguely.*) Roughly.

Guil (*clears his throat*) In the morning the sun would be easterly. I think we can assume that.

Ros That it's morning?

Guil If it is, and the sun is over *there* (*his right as he faces the audience*) for instance, *that* (*front*) would be northerly. On the other hand, if it is not morning and the sun is over *there* (*his left*) . . . *that* . . . (*lamely*) would *still* be northerly. (*Picking up.*) To put it another way, if we came from down there (*front*) and it is morning, the sun would be up there (*his left*), and if it is actually over *there* (*his right*) and it's still morning, we must have come from up *there* (*behind him*), and if *that* is southerly (*his left*) and the sun is really over *there* (*front*), then it's the afternoon. However, if none of these is the case –

Ros Why don't you go and have a look?

Guil Pragmatism?! – is that all you have to offer? You seem to have no conception of where we stand! You won't find the answer written down for you in the bowl of a compass – I can tell you that. (*Pause.*) Besides, you can never tell this far north – it's probably dark out there.

Ros I merely suggest that the position of the sun, if it is out, would give you a rough idea of the time; alternatively, the clock, if it is going, would give you a rough idea of the position of the sun. I forget which you're trying to establish.

Guil I'm trying to establish the direction of the wind.

Ros There isn't any wind. *Draught*, yes.

Guil In that case, the origin. Trace it to its source and it might give us a rough idea of the way we came in – which might give us a rough idea of south, for further reference.

Ros It's coming up through the floor. (*He studies the floor.*) That can't be south, can it?

Guil That's not a direction. Lick your toe and wave it around a bit.

Ros considers the distance of his foot.

Ros No, I think you'd have to lick it for me.

Pause.

Guil I'm prepared to let the whole matter drop.

Ros Or I could lick yours, of course.

Guil No thank you.

Ros I'll even wave it around for you.

Guil (*down Ros's throat*) What in God's name is the matter with you?

Ros Just being friendly.

Guil (*retiring*) Somebody might come in. It's what we're counting on, after all. Ultimately.

> *Good pause.*

Ros Perhaps they've all trampled each other to death in the rush . . . Give them a shout. Something provocative. *Intrigue* them.

Guil Wheels have been set in motion, and they have their own pace, to which we are . . . condemned. Each move is dictated by the previous one – that is the meaning of order. If we start being arbitrary it'll just be a shambles: at least, let us hope so. Because if we happened, just happened to discover, or even suspect, that our spontaneity was part of their order, we'd know that we were lost. (*He sits.*) A Chinaman of the T'ang Dynasty – and, by which definition, a philosopher – dreamed he was a butterfly, and from that moment he was never quite sure that he was not a butterfly dreaming it was a Chinese philosopher. Envy him; in his two-fold security.

> *A good pause. Ros leaps up and bellows at the audience.*

Ros Fire!

> *Guil jumps up.*

Guil Where?

Ros It's all right – I'm demonstrating the misuse of free speech. To prove that it exists. (*He regards the audience, that is the direction, with contempt – and other directions, then front again.*) Not a move. They should burn to death in their shoes.

> *Ros takes out one of his coins. Spins it. Catches it. Looks at it. Replaces it.*

Guil What was it?

Ros What?

Guil Heads or tails?

Ros Oh. I didn't look.

Guil Yes you did.

Ros Oh, did I? (*He takes out a coin, studies it.*) Quite right – it rings a bell.

Guil What's the last thing you remember?

Ros I don't wish to be reminded of it.

Guil We cross our bridges when we come to them and burn them behind us, with nothing to show for our progress except a memory of the smell of smoke, and a presumption that once our eyes watered.

> *Ros approaches him brightly, holding a coin between finger and thumb. He covers it with his other hand, draws his fists apart and holds them for Guil. Guil considers them. Indicates the left hand, Ros opens it to show it empty.*

Ros No.

> *Repeat process. Guil indicates left hand again. Ros shows it empty.*

Double bluff!

> *Repeat process – Guil taps one hand, then the other hand, quickly. Ros inadvertently shows that both are empty. Ros laughs as Guil turns upstage. Ros stops laughing, looks around his feet, pats his clothes, puzzled.*
> *Polonius breaks that up by entering upstage followed by the Tragedians and Hamlet.*

Polonius (*entering*) Come sirs.

Hamlet Follow him, friends. We'll hear a play tomorrow.

   Aside to the Player, who is the last of the Tragedians.

Dost thou hear me, old friend? Can you play 'The Murder of Gonzago'?

Player Ay, my lord.

Hamlet We'll ha't tomorrow night. You could for a need study a speech of some dozen or sixteen lines which I would set down and insert in't, could you not?

Player Ay, my lord.

Hamlet Very well. Follow that lord, and look you mock him not.

   The Player crossing downstage, notes Ros and Guil. Stops. Hamlet crossing downstage addresses them without pause.

Hamlet My good friends, I'll leave you till tonight. You are welcome to Elsinore.

Ros Good, my lord.

   Hamlet goes.

Guil So you've caught up.

Player (*coldly*) Not yet, sir.

Guil Now mind your tongue, or we'll have it out and throw the rest of you away, like a nightingale at a Roman feast.

Ros Took the very words out of my mouth.

Guil You'd be *lost* for words.

Ros You'd be tongue-tied.

Guil Like a mute in a monologue.

Ros Like a nightingale at a Roman feast.

Guil Your diction will go to pieces.

Ros Your lines will be cut.

Guil To dumbshows.

Ros And dramatic pauses.

Guil You'll never *find* your tongue.

Ros Lick your lips.

Guil Taste your tears.

Ros Your breakfast.

Guil You won't know the difference.

Ros There won't be any.

Guil We'll take the very words out of your mouth.

Ros So you've caught on.

Guil So you've caught up.

Player (*tops*) Not yet! (*bitterly*) You left us.

Guil Ah! I'd forgotten – you performed a dramatic spectacle on the way. Yes, I'm sorry we had to miss it.

Player (*bursts out*) We can't look each other in the face! (*Pause, more in control.*) You don't understand the humiliation of it – to be tricked out of the single assumption which makes our existence viable – that somebody is *watching* . . . The plot was two corpses gone before we caught sight of ourselves, stripped naked in the middle of nowhere and pouring ourselves down a bottomless well.

Ros Is *that* thirty-eight?

Player (*lost*) There we were – demented children mincing about in clothes that no one ever wore, speaking as no man ever spoke, swearing love in wigs and rhymed couplets, killing each other with wooden swords, hollow protestations of faith hurled after empty promises of vengeance – and every gesture, every pose, vanishing into the thin unpopulated air. We ransomed our dignity to the clouds, and the uncomprehending birds listened. (*He rounds on them.*) Don't you see?! We're *actors* – we're the opposite of people!

They recoil nonplussed, his voice calms.

Think, in your head, *now*, think of the most . . . *private* . . . *secret* . . . *intimate* thing you have ever done secure in the knowledge of its privacy . . .

He gives them – and the audience – a good pause. Ros takes on a shifty look.

Are you thinking of it? (*He strikes with his voice and his head.*) Well, I saw you do it!

Ros leaps up, dissembling madly.

Ros You never! It's a lie! (*He catches himself with a giggle in a vacuum and sits down again.*)

Player We're actors . . . We pledged our identities, secure in the conventions of our trade; that someone would be watching. And then, gradually, no one was. We were caught, high and dry. It was not until the murderer's long soliloquy that we were able to look around; frozen as we were in profile, our eyes searched you out, first confidently, then hesitantly, then desperately as each patch of turf, each log, every exposed corner in every direction proved uninhabited, and all the while the murderous King addressed the horizon with his dreary interminable guilt . . . Our heads began to move, wary as lizards, the corpse of unsullied Rosalinda peeped through his fingers, and the King faltered. Even then, habit and a stubborn trust that our audience spied upon us from behind the nearest bush, forced our bodies to blunder on long after they had emptied of meaning, until like runaway carts they dragged to a halt. No one came forward. No one shouted at us. The silence was unbreakable, it imposed itself upon us; it was obscene. We took off our crowns and swords and cloth of gold and moved silent on the road to Elsinore.

Silence. Then Guil claps solo with slow measured irony.

Guil Brilliantly re-created – if these eyes could weep! . . . Rather strong on metaphor, mind you. No criticism – only a matter of taste. And so here you are – with a vengeance. That's a figure of speech . . . isn't it? Well let's say we've made up for it, for you may have no doubt whom to thank for your performance at the court.

Ros We are counting on you to take him out of himself. You are the pleasures which we draw him on to – (*He escapes a fractional giggle but recovers immediately*.) and by that I don't mean your usual filth; you can't treat royalty like people with normal perverted desires. They know nothing of that and you know nothing of them, to your mutual survival. So give him a good clean show suitable for all the family, or you can rest assured you'll be playing the tavern tonight.

Guil Or the night after.

Ros Or not.

Player We already have an entry here. And always have had.

Guil You've played for him before?

Player Yes, sir.

Ros And what's *his* bent?

Player Classical.

Ros Saucy!

Guil What will you play?

Player 'The Murder of Gonzago'.

Guil Full of fine cadence and corpses.

Player Pirated from the Italian . . .

Ros What is it about?

Player It's about a King and Queen . . .

Guil Escapism! What else?

Player Blood –

Guil – Love and rhetoric.

Player Yes. (*Going.*)

Guil Where are you going?

Player I can come and go as I please.

Guil You're evidently a man who knows his way around.

Player I've been here before.

Guil We're still finding our feet.

Player I should concentrate on not losing your heads.

Guil Do you speak from knowledge?

Player Precedent.

Guil You've been here before.

Player And I know which way the wind is blowing.

Guil Operating on two levels, are we?! How clever! I

expect it comes naturally to you, being in the business so to speak.

The Player's grave face does not change. He makes to move off again. Guil for the second time cuts him off.

The truth is, we value your company, for want of any other. We have been left so much to our own devices – after a while one welcomes the uncertainty of being left to other people's.

Player Uncertainty is the normal state. You're nobody special.

He makes to leave again. Guil loses his cool.

Guil But for God's sake what are we supposed to *do*!

Player Relax. Respond. That's what people do. You can't go through life questioning your situation at every turn.

Guil But we don't know what's going on, or what to do with ourselves. We don't know how to *act*.

Player Act natural. You know why you're here at least.

Guil We only know what we're told, and that's little enough. And for all we know it isn't even true.

Player For all anyone knows, nothing is. Everything has to be taken on trust; truth is only that which is taken to be true. It's the currency of living. There may be nothing behind it, but it doesn't make any difference so long as it is honoured. One acts on assumptions. What do you assume?

Ros Hamlet is not himself, outside or in. We have to glean what afflicts him.

Guil He doesn't give much away.

Player Who does, nowadays?

Guil He's – melancholy.

Player Melancholy?

Ros Mad.

Player How is he mad?

Ros Ah. (*to Guil*) How is he mad?

Guil More morose than mad, perhaps.

Player Melancholy.

Guil Moody.

Ros He has moods.

Player Of moroseness?

Guil Madness. And yet.

Ros Quite.

Guil For instance.

Ros He talks to himself, which might be madness.

Guil If he didn't talk sense, which he does.

Ros Which suggests the opposite.

Player Of what?

  Small pause.

Guil I think I have it. A man talking sense to himself is no madder than a man talking nonsense not to himself.

Ros Or just as mad.

Guil Or just as mad.

Ros And he does both.

Guil So there you are.

Ros Stark raving sane.

  Pause.

Player Why?

Guil Ah. (*to Ros*) Why?

Ros Exactly.

Guil Exactly what?

Ros Exactly why.

Guil Exactly *why what*?

Ros What?

Guil *Why*?

Ros Why what, exactly?

Guil Why is he mad?!

Ros *I* don't know!

  Beat.

Player The old man thinks he's in love with his daughter.

Ros (*appalled*) Good God! We're out of our depth here.

Player No, no, no – *he* hasn't got a daughter – the old man thinks he's in love with *his* daughter.

Ros The old man is?

Player Hamlet, in love with the old man's daughter, the old man thinks.

Ros Ha! It's beginning to make sense! Unrequited passion!

  The Player moves.

Guil (*fascist*) Nobody leaves this room! (*Pause, lamely.*) Without a *very* good reason.

Player Why not?

Guil All this strolling about is getting too arbitrary by half – I'm rapidly losing my grip. From now on reason will prevail.

Player I have lines to learn.

Guil Pass!

> *The Player passes into one of the wings. Ros cups his hands and shouts into the opposite one.*

Ros Next!

> *But no one comes.*

Guil What did you expect?

Ros Something . . . someone . . . nothing.

> *They sit facing front.*

Are you hungry?

Guil No, are you?

Ros (*thinks*) No. You remember that coin.

Guil No.

Ros I think I lost it.

Guil What coin?

Ros I don't remember exactly.

> *Pause.*

Guil Oh, that coin . . . clever.

Ros I can't remember how I did it.

Guil It probably comes natural to you.

Ros Yes, I've got a show-stopper there.

Guil Do it again.

Slight pause.

Ros We can't afford it.

Guil Yes, one must think of the future.

Ros It's the normal thing.

Guil To have one. One is, after all, having it all the time . . . now . . . and now . . . and now . . .

Ros It could go on for ever. Well, not for *ever*, I suppose. (*Pause.*) Do you ever think of yourself as actually *dead*, lying in a box with a lid on it?

Guil No.

Ros Nor do I, really . . . It's silly to be depressed by it. I mean one thinks of it like being *alive* in a box, one keeps forgetting to take into account the fact that one is *dead* . . . which should make a difference . . . shouldn't it? I mean, you'd never *know* you were in a box, would you? It would be just like being *asleep* in a box. Not that I'd like to sleep in a box, mind you, not without any air – you'd wake up dead, for a start and then where would you be? Apart from inside a box. That's the bit I don't like, frankly. That's why I don't think of it . . .

Guil stirs restlessly, pulling his cloak round him.

Because you'd be helpless, wouldn't you? Stuffed in a box like that, I mean you'd be in there for ever. Even taking into account the fact that you're dead, really . . . *ask* yourself, if I asked you straight off – I'm going to stuff you in this box now, would you rather be alive or dead? Naturally, you'd prefer to be alive. Life in a box is better than no life at all. I expect. You'd have a chance at least. You could lie there thinking – well, at least I'm not dead! In a minute someone's going to bang on the lid and tell me to come out. (*Banging on the floor with his fists.*) 'Hey you, whatsyername! Come out of there!'

Guil (*jumps up savagely*) You don't have to flog it to death!

Pause.

Ros I wouldn't think about it, if I were you. You'd only get depressed. (*Pause.*) Eternity is a terrible thought. I mean, where's it going to end? (*Pause, then brightly.*) Two early Christians chanced to meet in Heaven. 'Saul of Tarsus yet!' cried one. 'What are *you* doing here?!' . . . 'Tarsus-Schmarsus', replied the other, 'I'm Paul already.' (*He stands up restlessly and flaps his arms.*) They don't care. We count for nothing. We could remain silent till we're green in the face, they wouldn't come.

Guil Blue, red.

Ros A Christian, a Moslem and a Jew chanced to meet in a closed carriage . . . 'Silverstein!' cried the Jew, 'Who's your friend?' . . . 'His name's Abdullah', replied the Moslem, 'but he's no friend of mine since he became a convert.' (*He leaps up again, stamps his foot and shouts into the wings.*) All right, we know you're in there! Come out talking! (*Pause.*) We have no control. None at all . . . (*He paces.*) Whatever became of the moment when one first knew about death? There must have been one, a moment, in childhood when it first occurred to you that you don't go on for ever. It must have been shattering – stamped into one's memory. And yet I can't remember it. It never occurred to me at all. What does one make of that? We must be born with an intuition of mortality. Before we know the words for it, before we know that there are words, out we come, bloodied and squalling with the knowledge that for all the compasses in the world, there's only one direction, and time is its only measure. (*He

reflects, getting more desperate and rapid.) A Hindu, a
Buddhist and a lion-tamer chanced to meet, in a circus on
the Indo-Chinese border. (*He breaks out.*) They're taking
us for granted! Well, I won't stand for it! In future, notice
will be taken. (*He wheels again to face into the wings.*)
Keep out, then! I forbid anyone to enter! (*No one comes –
Breathing heavily*) That's better . . .

> *Immediately, behind him a grand procession enters,
> principally Claudius, Gertrude, Polonius and Ophelia.
> Claudius takes Ros's elbow as he passes and is
> immediately deep in conversation: the context is
> Shakespeare Act III, scene i. Guil still faces front as
> Claudius, Ros, etc., pass upstage and turn.*

Guil Death followed by eternity . . . the worst of both
worlds. It *is* a terrible thought.

> *He turns upstage in time to take over the conversation
> with Claudius. Gertrude and Ros head downstage.*

Gertrude Did he receive you well?

Ros Most like a gentleman.

Guil (*returning in time to take it up*) But with much
forcing of his disposition.

Ros (*a flat lie and he knows it and shows it, perhaps
catching Guil's eye*) Niggard of question, but of our
demands most free in his reply.

Gertrude Did you assay him to any pastime?

Ros Madam, it so fell out that certain players
We o'erraught on the way: of these we told him
And there did seem in him a kind of joy
To hear of it. They are here about the court,
And, as I think, they have already order
This night to play before him.

Polonius 'Tis most true.
And he beseeched me to entreat your Majesties
To hear and see the matter.

Claudius With all my heart, and it doth content me
To hear him so inclined.
Good gentlemen, give him a further edge
And drive his purpose into these delights.

Ros We shall, my lord.

Claudius (*leading out procession*)
Sweet Gertrude, leave us, too,
For we have closely sent for Hamlet hither,
That he, as t'were by accident, may here
Affront Ophelia . . .

> *Exeunt Ophelia and Gertrude.*

Ros (*peevish*) Never a moment's peace! In and out, on and off, they're coming at us from all sides

Guil You're never satisfied.

Ros Catching us on the trot . . . Why can't *we* go by *them*?

Guil What's the difference?

Ros I'm going.

> *Ros pulls his cloak round him. Guil ignores him.*
> *Without confidence Ros heads upstage. He looks out*
> *and comes back quickly.*

He's coming.

Guil What's he doing?

Ros Nothing.

Guil He must be doing something.

Ros Walking.

Guil On his hands?

Ros No, on his feet.

Guil Stark naked?

Ros Fully dressed.

Guil Selling toffee apples?

Ros Not that I noticed.

Guil You could be wrong?

Ros I don't think so.

Pause.

Guil I can't for the life of me see how we're going to get into conversation.

Hamlet enters upstage, and pauses, weighing up the pros and cons of making his quietus.
Ros and Guil watch him.

Ros Nevertheless, I suppose one might say that this was a chance . . . One might well . . . accost him . . . Yes, it definitely looks like a chance to me . . . Something on the lines of a direct informal approach . . . man to man . . . straight from the shoulder . . . Now look here, what's it all about . . . sort of thing. Yes. Yes, this looks like one to be grabbed with both hands, I should say . . . if I were asked . . . No point in looking at a gift horse till you see the whites of its eyes, etcetera.

He moves towards Hamlet but his nerve fails. He returns.

We're overawed, that's our trouble. When it comes to the point we succumb to their personality.

Ophelia enters, with prayerbook, a religious procession of one.

Hamlet Nymph, in thy orisons be all my sins remembered.

At his voice she has stopped for him, he catches her up.

Ophelia Good my lord, how does your honour for this many a day?

Hamlet I humbly thank you – well, well, well.

They disappear talking into the wing.

Ros It's like living in a public park!

Guil Very impressive. Yes, I thought your direct informal approach was going to stop this thing dead in its tracks there. If I might make a suggestion – shut up and sit down. Stop being perverse.

Ros (*near tears*) I'm not going to stand for it!

A female figure, ostensibly the Queen, enters. Ros marches up behind her, puts his hands over her eyes and says with a desperate frivolity.

Guess who?!

Player (*having appeared in a downstage corner*) Alfred!

Ros lets go, spins around. He had been holding Alfred, in his robe and blond wig. The Player is in the downstage corner still. Ros comes down to that exit. The Player does not budge. He and Ros stand toe to toe.

Ros Excuse me.

The Player lifts his downstage foot. Ros bends to put his hand on the floor. The Player lowers his foot. Ros screams and leaps away.

Player (*gravely*) I beg your pardon.

Guil (*to Ros*) What did he do?

Player I put my foot down.

Ros My hand was on the floor!

Guil You put your hand under his foot?

Ros I –

Guil What for?

Ros I thought – (*Grabs Guil.*) Don't leave me!

He makes a break for an exit. A Tragedian dressed as a King enters. Ros recoils, breaks for the opposite wing. Two cloaked Tragedians enter. Ros tries again but another Tragedian enters, and Ros retires to midstage. The Player claps his hands matter-of-factly.

Player Right! We haven't got much time.

Guil What are you doing?

Player Dress rehearsal. Now if you two wouldn't mind just moving back . . . there . . . good . . . (*to the Tragedians*) Everyone ready? And for goodness sake, remember what we're doing. (*to Ros and Guil*) We always use the same costumes more or less, and they forget what they are supposed to be *in* you see . . . Stop picking your nose, Alfred. When Queens have to they do it by a cerebral process passed down in the blood . . . Good. Silence! Off we go!

Player-King Full thirty times hath Phoebus' cart –

The Player jumps up angrily.

Player No, no, no! Dumbshow first, your confounded majesty! (*to Ros and Guil*) They're a bit out of practice, but they always pick up wonderfully for the deaths – it brings out the poetry in them.

Guil How nice.

Player There's nothing more unconvincing than an unconvincing death.

Guil I'm sure.

The Player claps his hands.

Player Act One – moves now.

The mime. Soft music from a recorder. Player-King and Player-Queen embrace. She kneels and makes a show of protestation to him. He takes her up, declining his head upon her neck. He lies down. She, seeing him asleep, leaves him.

Guil What is the dumbshow for?

Player Well, it's a device, really – it makes the action that follows more or less comprehensible; you understand, we are tied down to a language which makes up in obscurity what it lacks in style.

The mime (continued) – enter another. He takes off the Sleeper's crown, kisses it. He had brought in a small bottle of liquid. He pours the poison in the Sleeper's ear, and leaves him. The Sleeper convulses heroically, dying.

Ros Who was that?

Player The King's brother and uncle to the Prince.

Guil Not exactly fraternal.

Player Not exactly avuncular, as time goes on.

The Queen returns, makes passionate action, finding the King dead. The Poisoner comes in again, attended by two others (the two in cloaks). The Poisoner seems to console with her. The dead body is carried away. The Poisoner woos the Queen with gifts. She seems harsh awhile but in

*the end accepts his love. End of mime, at which point, the
wail of a woman in torment and Ophelia appears,
wailing, closely followed by Hamlet in a hysterical state,
shouting at her, circling her, both midstage.*

Hamlet Go to, I'll no more on't; it hath made me mad!

She falls on her knees weeping.

I say we will have no more marriage! (*His voice drops to
include the Tragedians, who have frozen.*) Those that are
married already (*He leans close to the Player-Queen and
the Poisoner, speaking with quiet edge.*) all but one shall
live. (*He smiles briefly at them without mirth, and starts to
back out, his parting shot rising again.*) The rest shall keep
as they are. (*As he leaves, Ophelia tottering upstage, he
speaks into her ear a quick clipped sentence.*) To a
nunnery, go.

*He goes out. Ophelia falls on her knees upstage, her
sobs barely audible. A slight silence.*

Player-King Full thirty times hath Phoebus' cart –

*Claudius enters with Polonius and goes over to Ophelia
and lifts her to her feet. The Tragedians jump back with
heads inclined.*

Claudius Love? His affections do not that way tend,
Or what he spake, though it lacked form a little,
Was not like madness. There's something
in his soul o'er which his melancholy sits on
brood, and I do doubt the hatch and the
disclose will be some danger; which for to
prevent I have in quick determination thus set
it down: he shall with speed to England . . .

*Which carries the three of them – Claudius, Polonius,
Ophelia – out of sight. The Player moves, clapping his
hands for attention.*

Player Gentlemen! (*They look at him.*) It doesn't seem to be coming. We are not getting it at all. (*to Guil*) What did you think?

Guil What was I supposed to think?

Player (*to Tragedians*) You're not getting across!

Ros had gone half way up to Ophelia; he returns.

Ros That didn't look like love to me.

Guil Starting from scratch again . . .

Player (*to Tragedians*) It was a *mess*.

Ros (*to Guil*) It's going to be chaos on the night.

Guil Keep back – we're spectators.

Player Act two! Positions!

Guil Wasn't that the end?

Player Do you call that an ending? – with practically everyone on his feet? My goodness no – over your dead body.

Guil How am I supposed to take that?

Player Lying down. (*He laughs briefly and in a second has never laughed in his life.*) There's a design at work in all art – surely you know that? Events must play themselves out to aesthetic, moral and logical conclusion.

Guil And what's that, in this case?

Player It never varies – we aim at the point where everyone who is marked for death dies.

Guil Marked?

Player Between 'just deserts' and 'tragic irony' we are given quite a lot of scope for our particular talent.

Generally speaking, things have gone about as far as they can possibly go when things have got about as bad as they reasonably get. (*He switches on a smile.*)

Guil Who decides?

Player (*switching off his smile*) *Decides?* It is *written*.

(*He turns away. Guil grabs him and spins him back violently. Unflustered.*) Now if you're going to be subtle, we'll miss each other in the dark. I'm referring to oral tradition. So to speak.

Guil releases him.

We're tragedians, you see. We follow directions – there is no *choice* involved. The bad end unhappily, the good unluckily. That is what tragedy means. (*Calling*) Positions!

The Tragedians have taken up positions for the continuation of the mime: which in this case means a love scene, sexual and passionate, between the Queen and the Poisoner/King.

Player Go!

The lovers begin. The Player contributes a breathless commentary for Ros and Guil.

Having murdered his brother and wooed the widow – the poisoner mounts the throne! Here we see him and his queen give rein to their unbridled passion! She little knowing that the man she holds in her arms –!

Ros Oh, I say – here – really! You can't do that!

Player Why not?

Ros Well, really – I mean, people want to be *entertained* – they don't come expecting sordid and gratuitous filth.

Player You're wrong – they do! Murder, seduction and incest – what do you want – *jokes?*

Ros I want a good story, with a beginning, middle and end.

Player (*to Guil*) And you?

Guil I'd prefer art to mirror life, if it's all the same to you.

Player It's all the same to me, sir. (*to the grappling Lovers*) All right, no need to indulge yourselves. (*They get up – to Guil*) I come on in a minute. Lucianus, nephew to the king! (*Turns his attention to the Tragedians.*) Next!

They disport themselves to accommodate the next piece of mime, which consists of the Player himself exhibiting an excitable anguish (choreographed, stylized) leading to an impassioned scene with the Queen (cf. 'The Closet Scene', Shakespeare Act III, scene iv) and a very stylized reconstruction of a Polonius figure being stabbed behind the arras (the murdered King to stand in for Polonius) while the Player himself continues his breathless commentary for the benefit of Ros and Guil.

Player Lucianus, nephew to the king . . . usurped by his uncle and shattered by his mother's incestuous marriage . . . loses his reason . . . throwing the court into turmoil and disarray as he alternates between bitter melancholy and unrestricted lunacy . . . staggering from the suicidal (*a pose*) to the homicidal (*Here he kills 'Polonius'.*) . . . he at last confronts his mother and in a scene of provocative ambiguity – (*a somewhat oedipal embrace*) begs her to repent and recant –

He springs up, still talking.

The King – (*He pushes forward the Poisoner/King.*) tormented by guilt – haunted by fear – decides to despatch his nephew to England – and entrusts this undertaking to two smiling accomplices – friends – courtiers – to two spies –

He has swung round to bring together the Poisoner/

73

*King and the two cloaked Tragedians; the latter kneel
and accept a scroll from the King.*

– giving them a letter to present to the English court – !
And so they depart – on board ship –

*The two Spies position themselves on either side of the
Player, and the three of them sway gently in unison, the
motion of a boat; and then the Player detaches himself.*

– and they arrive –

One Spy shades his eyes at the horizon.

– and disembark – and present themselves before the
English King – (*He wheels round.*) The English King –

*An exchange of headgear creates the English King from
the remaining player – that is, the Player who played the
original murdered king.*

But where is the Prince? Where indeed? The plot has
thickened - a twist of fate and cunning has put into their
hands a letter that seals their deaths!

*The two Spies present their letter; the English King
reads it and orders their deaths. They stand up as the
Player whips off their cloaks preparatory to execution.*

Traitors hoist by their own petard? – or victims of the
Gods? – we shall never know!

*The whole mime has been fluid and continuous but now
Ros moves forward and brings it to a pause. What
brings Ros forward is the fact that under their cloaks
the two Spies are wearing coats identical to those worn
by Ros and Guil, whose coats are now covered by their
cloaks. Ros approaches 'his' Spy doubtfully. He does
not quite understand why the coats are familiar. Ros
stands close, touches the coat, thoughtfully . . .*

Ros Well, if it isn't –! No, wait a minute, don't tell me – it's a long time since – where was it? Ah, this is taking me back to – when was it? I know you, don't I? I never forget a face – (*He looks into the Spy's face.*) . . . not that I know yours that is. For a moment I thought – no, I don't know you, do I? Yes, I'm afraid you're quite wrong. You must have mistaken me for someone else.

Guil meanwhile has approached the other Spy, brow creased in thought.

Player (*to Guil*) Are you familiar with this play?

Guil No.

Player A slaughterhouse – eight corpses all told. It brings out the best in us.

Guil (*tense, progressively rattled during the whole mime and commentary*) You! – What do *you* know about *death*?

Player It's what the actors do best. They have to exploit whatever talent is given to them, and their talent is dying. They can die heroically, comically, ironically, slowly, suddenly, disgustingly, charmingly, or from a great height. My own talent is more general. I extract significance from melodrama, a significance which it does not in fact contain; but occasionally, from out of this matter, there escapes a thin beam of light that, seen at the right angle, can crack the shell of mortality.

Ros Is that all they can do – die?

Player No, no – they kill beautifully. In fact some of them kill even better than they die. The rest die better than they kill. They're a team.

Ros Which ones are which?

Player There's not much in it.

Guil (*fear, derision*) Actors! The mechanics of cheap melodrama! That isn't *death*! (*more quietly*) You scream and choke and sink to your knees, but it doesn't bring death home to anyone – it doesn't catch them unawares and start the whisper in their skulls that says – 'One day you are going to die.' (*He straightens up.*) You die so many times; how can you expect them to believe in your death?

Player On the contrary, it's the only kind they do believe. They're conditioned to it. I had an actor once who was condemned to hang for stealing a sheep – or a lamb, I forget which – so I got permission to have him hanged in the middle of a play – had to change the plot a bit but I thought it would be effective, you know – and you wouldn't believe it, he just *wasn't* convincing! It was impossible to suspend one's disbelief – and what with the audience jeering and throwing peanuts, the whole thing was a *disaster*! – he did nothing but cry all the time – right out of character – just stood there and cried . . . Never again.

> *In good humour he has already turned back to the mime: the two Spies awaiting execution at the hands of the Player.*

Audiences know what to expect, and that is all that they are prepared to believe in. (*to the Spies*) Show!

> *The Spies die at some length, rather well.*
> *The light has begun to go, and it fades as they die, and as Guil speaks.*

Guil No, no, no . . . you've got it all wrong . . . you can't act death. The *fact* of it is nothing to do with seeing it happen – it's not gasps and blood and falling about – that isn't what makes it death. It's just a man failing to reappear, that's all – now you see him, now you don't, that's the only thing that's real: here one minute and gone the next and never coming back – an exit, unobtrusive and unannounced, a disappearance gathering weight as it goes on, until, finally, it is heavy with death.

> *The two Spies lie still, barely visible. The Player comes forward and throws the spies' cloaks over their bodies. Ros starts to clap, slowly.*
>
> *Blackout.*
>
> *A second of silence, then much noise. Shouts . . . 'The King rises!' . . . 'Give o'er the play!' . . . and cries for 'Lights, lights, lights!'*
>
> *When the light comes, after a few seconds, it comes as a sunrise. The stage is empty save for two cloaked Figures sprawled on the ground in the approximate positions last held by the dead Spies. As the light grows, they are seen to be Ros and Guil, and to be resting quite comfortably. Ros raises himself on his elbows and shades his eyes as he stares into the auditorium. Finally:*

Ros That must be east, then. I think we can assume that.

Guil I'm assuming nothing.

Ros No, it's all right. That's the sun. East.

Guil (*looks up*) Where?

Ros I watched it come up.

Guil No . . . it was light all the time, you see, and you opened your eyes very, very slowly. If you'd been facing back there you'd be swearing *that* was east.

Ros (*standing up*) You're a mass of prejudice.

Guil I've been taken in before.

Ros (*looks out over the audience*) Rings a bell.

Guil They're waiting to see what we're going to do.

Ros Good old east.

Guil As soon as we make a move they'll come pouring in from every side, shouting obscure instructions, confusing us with ridiculous remarks, messing us about from here to breakfast and getting our names wrong.

Ros starts to protest but he has hardly opened his mouth before:

Claudius (*off-stage – with urgency*) Ho, Guildenstern!

Guil is still prone. Small pause.

Ros and Guil You're wanted . . .

Guil furiously leaps to his feet as Claudius and Gertrude enter. They are in some desperation.

Claudius Friends both, go join you with some further aid: Hamlet in madness hath Polonius slain, and from his mother's closet hath he dragged him. Go seek him out; speak fair and bring the body into the chapel. I pray you haste in this. (*As he and Gertrude are hurrying out.*) Come, Gertrude, we'll call up our wisest friends and let them know both what we mean to do . . .

They've gone.
  Ros and Guil remain quite still.

Guil Well . . .

Ros Quite . . .

Guil Well, well.

Ros Quite; quite. (*Nods with spurious confidence.*) Seek him out. (*Pause.*) Etcetera.

Guil Quite.

Ros Well. (*Small pause.*) Well, that's a step in the right direction.

Guil You didn't like him?

Ros Who?

Guil Good God, I hope more tears are shed for *us*! . . .

Ros Well, it's *progress*, isn't it? Something positive. Seek him out. (*Looks round without moving his feet.*) Where does one begin . . .? (*Takes one step towards the wings and halts.*)

Guil Well, that's a step in the right direction.

Ros You think so? He could be anywhere.

Guil All right – you go that way, I'll go this way.

Ros Right.

> *They walk towards opposite wings. Ros halts.*

No.

> *Guil halts.*

You go this way – I'll go that way.

Guil All right.

> *They march towards each other, cross. Ros halts.*

Ros Wait a minute.

> *Guil halts.*

I think we should stick together. He might be violent.

Guil Good point. I'll come with you.

> *Guil marches across to Ros. They turn to leave. Ros halts.*

Ros No, I'll come with *you*.

Guil Right.

> *They turn, march across to the opposite wing. Ros halts. Guil halts.*

Ros I'll come with *you, my* way.

Guil All right.

They turn again and march across. Ros halts. Guil halts.

Ros I've just thought. If we both go, he could come *here*. That would be stupid, wouldn't it?

Guil All right – I'll stay, you go.

Ros Right.

Guil marches to midstage.

I say.

Guil wheels and carries on marching back towards Ros who starts marching downstage. They cross. Ros halts.

I've just thought.

Guil halts.

We ought to stick together; he might be violent.

Guil Good point.

Guil marches down to join Ros. They stand still for a moment in their original positions.

Well, at last we're getting somewhere.

Pause.

Guil Of course, he might not come.

Ros (*airily*) Oh, he'll come.

Guil We'd have some explaining to do.

Ros He'll come. (*Airily wanders upstage.*) Don't worry – take my word for it – (*Looks out – is appalled.*) He's coming!

Guil What's he doing?

Ros Walking.

Guil Alone?

Ros No.

Guil Who's with him?

Ros The old man.

Guil Walking?

Ros No.

Guil Not walking?

Ros No.

Guil Ah. That's an opening if ever there was one. (*And is suddenly galvanized into action.*) Let him walk into the trap!

Ros What trap?

Guil You stand there! Don't let him pass!

He positions Ros with his back to one wing, facing Hamlet's entrance.

Guil positions himself next to Ros, a few feet away, so that they are covering one side of the stage, facing the opposite side. Guil unfastens his belt. Ros does the same. They join the two belts, and hold them taut between them. Ros's trousers slide slowly down. Hamlet enters opposite, slowly, dragging Polonius's body. He enters upstage, makes a small arc and leaves by the same side, a few feet downstage.

Ros and Guil, holding the belts taut, stare at him in some bewilderment.

Hamlet leaves, dragging the body. They relax the strain on the belts.

Ros That was close.

Guil There's a limit to what two people can do.

They undo the belts: Ros pulls up his trousers.

Ros (*worriedly – he walks a few paces towards Hamlet's exit*) He *was* dead.

Guil Of course he's dead!

Ros (*turns to Guil*) Properly.

Guil (*angrily*) Death's death, isn't it?

Ros falls silent. Pause.

Perhaps he'll come back this way.

Ros starts to take off his belt.

No, no, no! – if we can't learn by experience, what else have we got?

Ros desists. Pause.

Ros Give him a shout.

Guil I thought we'd been into all that.

Ros (*shouts*) Hamlet!

Guil Don't be absurd.

Ros (*shouts*) Lord Hamlet!

Hamlet enters. Ros is a little dismayed.

What have you done, my lord, with the dead body?

Hamlet Compounded it with dust, whereto 'tis kin.

Ros Tell us where 'tis, that we may take it thence and bear it to the chapel.

Hamlet Do not believe it.

Ros Believe what?

Hamlet That I can keep your counsel and not mine own. Besides, to be demanded of a sponge, what replication should be made by the son of a king?

Ros Take you me for a sponge, my lord?

Hamlet Ay, sir, that soaks up the King's countenance, his rewards, his authorities. But such officers do the King best service in the end. He keeps them, like an ape, in the corner of his jaw, first mouthed, to be last swallowed. When he needs what you have gleaned, it is but squeezing you and, sponge, you shall be dry again.

Ros I understand you not, my lord.

Hamlet I am glad of it: a knavish speech sleeps in a foolish ear.

Ros My lord, you must tell us where the body is and go with us to the King.

Hamlet The body is with the King, but the King is not with the body. The King is a thing –

Guil A thing, my lord – ?

Hamlet Of nothing. Bring me to him.

Hamlet moves resolutely towards one wing. They move with him, shepherding. Just before they reach the exit, Hamlet, apparently seeing Claudius approaching from off stage, bends low in a sweeping bow. Ros and Guil, cued by Hamlet, also bow deeply – a sweeping ceremonial bow with their cloaks swept round them. Hamlet, however, continues the movement into an about-turn and walks off in the opposite direction. Ros and Guil, with their heads low, do not notice. No one comes on. Ros and Guil squint upwards and find that they are bowing to nothing.

Claudius enters behind them. At his first words they leap up and do a double-take.

Claudius How now? What hath befallen?

Ros Where the body is bestowed, my lord, we cannot get from him.

Claudius But where is he?

Ros (*fractional hesitation*) Without, my lord; guarded to know your pleasure.

Claudius (*moves*) Bring him before us.

> *This hits Ros between the eyes but only his eyes show it. Again his hesitation is fractional. And then with great deliberation he turns to Guil.*

Ros Ho! Bring in the lord.

> *Again there is a fractional moment in which Ros is smug, Guil is trapped and betrayed. Guil opens his mouth and closes it.*
> *The situation is saved:*
> *Hamlet, escorted, is marched in just as Claudius leaves.*
> *Hamlet and his Escort cross the stage and go out, following Claudius.*
> *Lighting changes to exterior.*

Ros (*moves to go*) All right, then?

Guil (*does not move: thoughtfully*) And yet it doesn't seem enough; to have breathed such significance. Can that be all? And why us? – anybody would have done. And we have contributed nothing.

Ros It was a trying episode while it lasted, but they've done with us now.

Guil Done what?

Ros I don't pretend to have understood. Frankly, I'm not very interested. If they won't tell us, that's their affair. (*He wanders upstage towards the exit.*) For my part, I'm only glad that that's the last we've seen of him –

And he glances offstage and turns front, his face betraying the fact that Hamlet is there.

Guil I knew it wasn't the end . . .

Ros (*high*) What else?!

Guil We're taking him to England. What's he doing?

Ros goes upstage and returns.

Ros Talking.

Guil To himself?

Ros makes to go, Guil cuts him off.

Is he alone?

Ros No, he's with a soldier.

Guil Then he's not talking to himself, is he?

Ros Not *by* himself . . . Should we go?

Guil Where?

Ros Anywhere.

Guil Why?

Ros puts up his head listening.

Ros There it is again. (*in anguish*) All I ask is a change of ground!

Guil (*coda*) Give us this day our daily round . . .

Hamlet enters behind them, talking with a soldier in arms. Ros and Guil don't look round.

Ros They'll have us hanging about till we're dead. At

least. And the weather will change. (*Looks up.*) The spring can't last for ever.

Hamlet Good sir, whose powers are these?

Soldier They are of Norway, sir.

Hamlet How purposed, sir, I pray you?

Soldier Against some part of Poland.

Hamlet Who commands them, sir?

Soldier The nephew to old Norway, Fortinbras.

Ros We'll be cold. The summer won't last.

Guil It's autumnal.

Ros (*examining the ground*) No leaves.

Guil Autumnal – nothing to do with leaves. It is to do with a certain brownness at the edges of the day . . . Brown is creeping up on us, take my word for it . . . Russets and tangerine shades of old gold flushing the very outside edge of the senses . . . deep shining ochres, burnt umber and parchments of baked earth – reflecting on itself and through itself, filtering the light. At such times, perhaps, coincidentally, the leaves might fall, somewhere, by repute. Yesterday was blue, like smoke.

Ros (*head up, listening*) I got it again then.

They listen – faintest sound of the Tragedians' band.

Hamlet I humbly thank you, sir.

Soldier God by you, sir. (*Exit.*)

Ros gets up quickly and goes to Hamlet.

Ros Will it please you go, my lord?

Hamlet I'll be with you straight. Go you a little before.

Hamlet turns to face upstage. Ros returns down. Guil faces front, doesn't turn.

Guil Is he there?

Ros Yes.

Guil What's he doing?

Ros looks over his shoulder.

Ros Talking.

Guil To himself?

Ros Yes. (*Pause. He makes to leave.*)

He *said* we can go. Cross my heart.

Guil I like to know where I am. Even if I don't know where I am, I like to know *that*. If we go there's no knowing.

Ros No knowing what?

Guil If we'll ever come back.

Ros We don't want to come back.

Guil That may very well be true, but do we want to go?

Ros We'll be free.

Guil I don't know. It's the same sky.

Ros We've come this far.

He moves towards exit. Guil follows him.

And besides, anything could happen yet.

They go.

Blackout.

Act Three

Opens in pitch darkness.
  Soft sea sounds.
  After several seconds of nothing, a voice from the dark . . .

Guil Are you there?

Ros Where?

Guil (*bitterly*) A flying start . . .

  Pause.

Ros Is that you?

Guil Yes.

Ros How do you know?

Guil (*explosion*) Oh-for-God's-sake!

Ros We're not finished, then?

Guil Well, we're here, aren't we?

Ros Are we? I can't see a thing.

Guil You can still *think*, can't you?

Ros I think so.

Guil You can still *talk*.

Ros What should I say?

Guil Don't bother. You can *feel*, can't you?

Ros Ah! There's life in me yet!

Guil What are you feeling?

Ros A leg. Yes, it feels like my leg.

Guil How does it feel?

Ros Dead.

Guil Dead?

Ros (*panic*) I can't feel a thing!

Guil Give it a pinch! (*Immediately he yelps.*)

Ros Sorry.

Guil Well, that's cleared that up.

Longer pause: the sound builds a little and identifies itself – the sea. Ship timbers, wind in the rigging, and then shouts of sailors calling obscure but inescapably nautical instructions from all directions, far and near: A short list:

Hard a larboard!
Let go the stays!
Reef down me hearties!
Is that you, cox'n?
Hel-llo! Is that you?
Hard a port!
Easy as she goes!
Keep her steady on the lee!
Haul away, lads!
(*Snatches of sea shanty maybe.*)
Fly the jib!
Tops'l up, me maties!

When the point has been well made and more so.

Ros We're on a boat. (*Pause.*) Dark, isn't it?

Guil Not for night.

Ros No, not for *night*.

Guil Dark for day.

Pause.

Ros Oh yes, it's dark for *day*.

Guil We must have gone north, of course.

Ros Off course?

Guil Land of the midnight sun, that is.

Ros Of course.

> *Some sailor sounds.*
> *A lantern is lit upstage – in fact by Hamlet.*
> *The stage lightens disproportionately.*
> *Enough to see:*
> *Ros and Guil sitting downstage.*
> *Vague shapes of rigging, etc., behind.*

I think it's getting light.

Guil Not for night.

Ros This far north.

Guil Unless we're off course.

Ros (*small pause*) Of course.

> *A better light – Lantern? Moon? . . . Light.*
> *Revealing, among other things, three large man-sized casks on deck, upended, with lids. Spaced but in line.*
> *Behind and above – a gaudy striped umbrella, on a pole stuck into the deck, tilted so that we do not see behind it – one of those huge six-foot diameter jobs.*
> *Still dim upstage.*
> *Ros and Guil still facing front.*

Ros Yes, it's lighter than it was. It'll be night soon. This far north. (*dolefully*) I suppose we'll have to go to sleep. (*He yawns and stretches.*)

Guil Tired?

Ros No . . . I don't think I'd take to it. Sleep all night, can't see a thing all day . . . Those eskimos must have a quiet life.

Guil Where?

Ros What?

Guil I thought you – (*Relapses.*) I've lost all capacity for disbelief. I'm not sure that I could even rise to a little gentle scepticism.

   Pause.

Ros Well, shall we stretch our legs?

Guil I don't feel like stretching my legs.

Ros I'll stretch them for you, if you like.

Guil No.

Ros We could stretch each other's. That way we wouldn't have to go anywhere.

Guil (*pause*) No, somebody might come in.

Ros In where?

Guil Out here.

Ros In out here?

Guil On deck.

   Ros considers the floor: slaps it.

Ros Nice bit of planking, that.

Guil Yes, I'm very fond of boats myself. I like the way they're – contained. You don't have to worry about which way to go, or whether to go at all – the question doesn't arise, because you're on a *boat*, aren't you? Boats are safe areas in the game of tag . . . the players will hold their positions until the music starts . . . I think I'll spend most of my life on boats.

Ros Very healthy.

Ros inhales with expectation, exhales with boredom. Guil stands up and looks over the audience.

Guil One is free on a boat. For a time. Relatively.

Ros What's it like?

Guil Rough.

Ros joins him. They look out over the audience.

Ros I think I'm going to be sick.

Guil licks a finger, holds it up experimentally.

Guil Other side, I think.

Ros goes upstage: Ideally a sort of upper deck joined to the downstage lower deck by short steps. The umbrella being on the upper deck. Ros pauses by the umbrella and looks behind it.

Guil meanwhile has been resuming his own theme – looking out over the audience –

Free to move, speak, extemporise, and yet. We have not been cut loose. Our truancy is defined by one fixed star, and our drift represents merely a slight change of angle to it: we may seize the moment, toss it around while the moments pass, a short dash here, an exploration there, but we are brought round full circle to face again the single immutable fact – that we, Rosencrantz and Guildenstern, bearing a letter from one king to another, are taking Hamlet to England.

By which time, Ros has returned, tiptoeing with great import, teeth clenched for secrecy, gets to Guil, points surreptitiously behind him – and a tight whisper:

Ros I say – *he's there*!

Guil (*unsurprised*) What's he doing?

Ros Sleeping.

Guil It's all right for him.

Ros What is?

Guil He can sleep.

Ros It's all right for him.

Guil He's got us now.

Ros He can sleep.

Guil It's all done for him.

Ros He's got us.

Guil And we've got nothing. (*a cry*) All I ask is our common due!

Ros For those in peril on the sea . . .

Guil Give us this day our daily cue.

Beat, pause. Sit. Long pause.

Ros (*after shifting, looking around*) What now?

Guil What do you mean?

Ros Well, nothing is happening.

Guil We're on a boat.

Ros I'm aware of that.

Guil (*angrily*) Then what do you expect? (*unhappily*) We act on scraps of information . . . sifting half-remembered directions that we can hardly separate from instinct.

> *Ros puts a hand into his purse, then both hands behind his back, then holds his fists out.*
> *Guil taps one fist.*
> *Ros opens it to show a coin.*
> *He gives it to Guil.*
> *He puts his hand back into his purse. Then both hands behind his back, then holds his fists out.*
> *Guil taps one.*
> *Ros opens it to show a coin. He gives it to Guil.*
> *Repeat.*
> *Repeat.*
> *Guil getting tense. Desperate to lose.*
> *Repeat.*
> *Guil taps a hand, changes his mind, taps the other, and Ros inadvertently reveals that he has a coin in both fists.*

Guil You had money in both hands.

Ros (*embarrassed*) Yes.

Guil Every time?

Ros Yes.

Guil What's the point of that?

Ros (*pathetic*) I wanted to make you happy.

> *Beat.*

Guil How much did he give you?

Ros Who?

Guil The King. He gave us some money.

Ros How much did he give you?

Guil I asked you first.

Ros I got the same as you.

Guil He wouldn't discriminate between us.

Ros How much did you get?

Guil The same.

Ros How do you know?

Guil You just told me – how do *you* know?

Ros He wouldn't discriminate between us.

Guil Even if he could.

Ros Which he never could.

Guil He couldn't even be sure of mixing us up.

Ros Without mixing us up.

Guil (*turning on him furiously*) Why don't you say something original! No wonder the whole thing is so stagnant! You don't take me up on anything – you just repeat it in a different order.

Ros I can't think of anything original. I'm only good in support.

Guil I'm sick of making the running.

Ros (*humbly*) It must be your dominant personality. (*almost in tears*) Oh, what's going to become of us! (*And Guil comforts him, all harshness gone.*)

Guil Don't cry . . . it's all right . . . there . . . there, I'll see we're all right.

Ros But we've got nothing to go on, we're out on our own.

Guil We're on our way to England – we're taking Hamlet there.

Ros What for?

Guil What for? Where have you been?

Ros When? (*Pause.*) We won't know what to do when we get there.

Guil We take him to the King.

Ros Will *he* be there?

Guil No – the King of England.

Ros He's expecting us?

Guil No.

Ros He won't know what we're playing at. What are we going to *say*?

Guil We've got a letter. You remember the letter.

Ros Do I?

Guil Everything is explained in the letter. We count on that.

Ros Is that it, then?

Guil What?

Ros We take Hamlet to the English King, we hand over the letter – what then?

Guil There may be something in the letter to keep us going a bit.

Ros And if not?

Guil Then that's it – we're finished.

Ros At a loose end?

Guil Yes.

Pause.

Ros Are there likely to be loose ends? (*Pause.*) Who is the English King?

Guil That depends on when we get there.

Ros What do you think it says?

Guil Oh . . . greetings. Expressions of loyalty. Asking of favours, calling in of debts. Obscure promises balanced by vague threats . . . Diplomacy. Regards to the family.

Ros And about Hamlet?

Guil Oh *yes*.

Ros And us – the full background?

Guil I should say so.

Pause.

Ros So we've got a letter which explains everything.

Guil You've got it.

Ros takes that literally. He starts to pat his pockets, etc.

What's the matter?

Ros The letter.

Guil Have you got it?

Ros (*rising fear*) Have I? (*Searches frantically.*) Where would I have put it?

Guil You can't have lost it.

Ros I must have!

Guil That's odd – I thought he gave it to me.

Ros looks at him hopefully.

Ros Perhaps he did.

Guil But you seemed so sure it was *you* who hadn't got it.

Ros (*high*) It *was* me who hadn't got it!

Guil But if he gave it to me there's no reason why you should have had it in the first place, in which case I don't see what all the fuss is about you *not* having it.

Ros (*pause*) I admit it's confusing.

Guil This is all getting rather undisciplined . . . The boat, the night, the sense of isolation and uncertainty . . . all these induce a loosening of the concentration. We must not lose control. Tighten up. Now. Either you have lost the letter or you didn't have it to lose in the first place, in which case the king never gave it to you, in which case he gave it to me, in which case I would have put it into my inside top pocket in which case (*Calmly producing the letter.*) . . . it will be . . . here. (*They smile at each other.*) We mustn't drop off like that again.

    Pause. Ros takes the letter gently from him.

Ros Now that we have found it, why were we looking for it?

Guil (*thinks*) We thought it was lost.

Ros Something else?

Guil No.

    Deflation.

Ros Now we've lost the tension.

Guil What tension?

Ros What was the last thing I said before we wandered off?

Guil When was that?

Ros (*helplessly*) I can't remember.

Guil (*leaping up*) What a shambles! We're just not getting anywhere.

Ros (*mournfully*) Not even England. I don't believe in it anyway.

Guil What?

Ros England.

Guil Just a conspiracy of cartographers, you mean?

Ros I mean I don't believe it! (*calmer*) I have no image. I try to picture us arriving, a little harbour perhaps . . . roads . . . inhabitants to point the way . . . horses on the road . . . riding for a day or a fortnight and then a palace and the English King . . . That would be the logical kind of thing . . . But my mind remains a blank. No. We're slipping off the map.

Guil Yes . . . yes . . . (*Rallying.*) But you don't believe anything till it happens. As it *has* all happened. Hasn't it?

Ros We drift down time, clutching at straws. But what good's a brick to a drowning man?

Guil Don't give up, we can't be long now.

Ros We might as well be dead. Do you think death could possibly be a boat?

Guil No, no, no . . . Death is . . . not. Death isn't. You take my meaning. Death is the ultimate negative. Not-being. You can't not-be on a boat.

Ros I've frequently not been on boats.

Guil No, no, no – what you've been is not on boats.

Ros I wish I was dead. (*Considering the drop.*) I could jump over the side. That would put a spoke in their wheel.

Guil Unless they're counting on it.

Ros I shall remain on board. That'll put a spoke in their wheel. (*the futility of it, fury*) All right! We don't question, we don't doubt. We perform. But a line must be drawn somewhere, and I would like to put it on record that I have no confidence in England. Thank you. (*Thinks about this.*) And even if it's true, it'll be another shambles.

Guil I don't see why.

Ros (*furious*) He won't know what we're talking about – What are we going to *say*?

Guil We say – Your majesty, we have arrived!

Ros (*kingly*) And who are you?

Guil We are Rosencrantz and Guildenstern.

Ros (*barks*) Never heard of you!

Guil Well, we're nobody special –

Ros (*regal and nasty*) What's your game?

Guil We've got our instructions –

Ros First I've heard of it –

Guil (*angrily*) Let me finish – (*humble*) We've come from Denmark.

Ros What do you want?

Guil Nothing – we're delivering Hamlet –

Ros Who's he?

Guil (*irritated*) You've heard of *him* –

Ros Oh, I've heard of him all right and I want nothing to do with it.

Guil But –

Ros You march in here without so much as a by your leave and expect me to take every lunatic you try to pass off with a lot of unsubstantiated –

Guil We've got a letter –

Ros snatches it and tears it open.

Ros (*efficiently*) I see . . . I see . . . well, this seems to support your story such as it is – it is an exact command from the King of Denmark, for several different reasons, importing Denmark's health and England's too, that on the reading of this letter, without delay, I should have Hamlet's head cut off –!

Guil snatches the letter. Ros, doubletaking, snatches it back, Guil snatches it half back. They read it together, and separate. Pause.
They are well downstage looking front.

Ros The sun's going down. It will be dark soon.

Guil Do you think so?

Ros I was just making conversation. (*Pause.*) We're his *friends*.

Guil How do you know?

Ros From our young days brought up with him.

Guil You've only got their word for it.

Ros But that's what we depend on.

Guil Well, yes, and then again no. (*airily*) Let us keep things in proportion. Assume, if you like, that they're going to kill him. Well, he is a man, he is mortal, death comes to us all, etcetera, and consequently he would have died anyway, sooner or later. Or to look at it from the social point of view – he's just one man among many, the loss would be well within reason and convenience. And then again, what is so terrible about death? As Socrates so philosophically put it, since we don't know what death is, it is illogical to fear it. It might be . . . very nice. Certainly it is a release from the burden of life, and, for the godly, a haven and a reward. Or to look at it another way – we are little men, we don't know the ins and outs of the matter, there are wheels within wheels, etcetera – it would be presumptuous of us to interfere with the design of fate or even of kings. All in all, I think we'd be well advised to leave well alone. Tie up the letter – there – neatly – like that – They won't notice the broken seal, assuming you were in character.

Ros But what's the point?

Guil Don't apply logic.

Ros He's done nothing to us.

Guil Or justice.

Ros It's awful.

Guil But it could have been worse. I was beginning to think it was.

> *And his relief comes out in a laugh. Behind them Hamlet appears from behind the umbrella. The light has been going. Slightly. Hamlet is going to the lantern.*

Ros The position as I see it, then. We, Rosencrantz and Guildenstern, from our young days brought up with him, awakened by a man standing on his saddle, are summoned, and arrive, and are instructed to glean what afflicts him and draw him on to pleasures, such as a play, which unfortunately, as it turns out, is abandoned in some confusion owing to certain nuances outside our appreciation – which, among other causes, results in, among other effects, a high, not to say, homicidal, excitement in Hamlet, whom we, in consequence, are escorting, for his own good, to England. Good. We're on top of it now.

> *Hamlet blows out the lantern. The stage goes pitch black. The black resolves itself to moonlight, by which Hamlet approaches the sleeping Ros and Guil. He extracts the letter and takes it behind his umbrella; the light of his lantern shines through the fabric, Hamlet emerges again with a letter, and replaces it, and retires, blowing out his lantern.*
>
> *Morning comes.*
>
> *Ros watches it coming – from the auditorium. Behind him is a gay sight. Beneath the re-tilted umbrella, reclining in a deckchair, wrapped in a rug, reading a book, possibly smoking, sits Hamlet.*
>
> *Ros watches the morning come, and brighten to high noon.*

Ros I'm assuming nothing. (*He stands up. Guil wakes.*) The position as I see it, then. That's west unless we're off course, in which case it's night; the King gave me the same as you, the King gave you the same as me; the King never gave me the letter, the King gave you the letter, we don't know what's in the letter; we take Hamlet to the English King, it depending on when we get there who he is, and we hand over the letter, which may or may not have something in it to keep us going, and if not, we are finished and at a loose end. We could have done worse. I don't think we missed any chances . . . Not that we're getting much help. (*He sits down again. They lie down – prone.*) If we stopped breathing we'd vanish.

> *The muffled sound of a recorder. They sit up with disproportionate interest.*

Here we go.
   Yes, but what?

They listen to the music.

Guil (*excitedly*) Out of the void, finally, a sound; while on a boat (admittedly) outside the action (admittedly) the perfect and absolute silence of the wet lazy slap of water against water and the rolling creak of timber – breaks; giving rise at once to the speculation or the assumption or the hope that something is about to happen; a pipe is heard. One of the sailors has pursed his lips against a woodwind, his fingers and thumb governing, shall we say, the ventages, whereupon, giving it breath, let us say, with his mouth, it, the pipe, discourses, as the saying goes, most eloquent music. A thing like that, it could change the course of events. (*Pause.*) Go and see what it is.

Ros It's someone playing on a pipe.

Guil Go and find him.

Ros And then what?

Guil I don't know – request a tune.

Ros What for?

Guil Quick – before we lose our momentum.

Ros Why! – something is happening. It had quite escaped my attention!

He listens: Makes a stab at an exit. Listens more carefully:
Changes direction:
Guil takes no notice.
Ros wanders about trying to decide where the music comes from. Finally he tracks it down – unwillingly – to the middle barrel. There is no getting away from it. He turns to Guil who takes no notice. Ros, during this whole business, never quite breaks into articulate speech. His face and his hands indicate his incredulity. He stands gazing at the middle barrel. The pipe plays on

*within. He kicks the barrel. The pipe stops. He leaps
back towards Guil. The pipe starts up again. He
approaches the barrel cautiously. He lifts the lid. The
music is louder. He slams down the lid. The music is
softer. He goes back towards Guil. But a drum starts,
muffled. He freezes. He turns. Considers the left-hand
barrel. The drumming goes on within, in time to the
flute. He walks back to Guil. He opens his mouth to
speak. Doesn't make it. A lute is heard. He spins round
at the third barrel. More instruments join in. Until it is
quite inescapable that inside the three barrels,
distributed, playing together a familiar tune which has
been heard three times before, are the Tragedians.*
 They play on.
 Ros sits beside Guil. They stare ahead.
 The tune comes to an end.
 Pause.

Ros I thought I heard a band. (*in anguish*) Plausibility is
all I presume!

Guil (*coda*) Call us this day our daily tune . . .

*The lid of the middle barrel flies open and the Player's
head pops out.*

Player Aha! All in the same boat, then! (*He climbs out. He
goes round banging on the barrels.*) Everybody out!

*Impossibly, the Tragedians climb out of the barrels.
With their instruments, but not their cart. A few
bundles. Except Alfred. The Player is cheerful.*
 To Ros:

Where are we?

Ros Travelling.

Player Of course, we haven't got there yet.

Ros Are we all right for England?

Player You look all right to me. I don't think they're very particular in England. Al-l-fred!

Alfred emerges from the Player's barrel.

Guil What are you doing here?

Player Travelling. (*to Tragedians*) Right – blend into the background!

The Tragedians are in costume (from the mime): A King with crown, Alfred as Queen, the Poisoner and the two Cloaked figures.
They blend.
To Guil:

Pleased to see us? (*Pause.*) You've come out of it very well, so far.

Guil And you?

Player In disfavour. Our play offended the King.

Guil Yes.

Player Well, he's a second husband himself. Tactless, really.

Ros It was quite a good play nevertheless.

Player We never really got going – it was getting quite interesting when they stopped it. (*Looks up at Hamlet.*) That's the way to travel . . .

Guil What were you doing in there?

Player Hiding. (*Indicating costumes*) We had to run for it just as we were.

Ros Stowaways.

Player Naturally – we didn't get paid, owing to circumstances ever so slightly beyond our control, and all the money we had we lost betting on certainties. Life is a gamble, at terrible odds – if it was a bet you wouldn't take it. Did you know that any number doubled is even?

Ros Is it?

Player We learn something every day, to our cost. But we troupers just go on and on. Do you know what happens to old actors?

Ros What?

Player Nothing. They're still acting. Surprised, then?

Guil What?

Player Surprised to see us?

Guil I knew it wasn't the end.

Player With practically everyone on his feet. What do you make of it, so far?

Guil We haven't got much to go on.

Player You speak to him?

Ros It's possible.

Guil But it wouldn't make any difference.

Ros But it's possible.

Guil Pointless.

Ros It's allowed.

Guil Allowed, yes. We are not restricted. No boundaries have been defined, no inhibitions imposed. We have, for the while, secured, or blundered into, our release, for the while. Spontaneity and whim are the order of the day. Other wheels are turning but they are not our concern. We can breathe. We can relax. We can do what we like and say what we like to whomever we like, without restriction.

Ros Within limits, of course.

Guil Certainly within limits.

Hamlet comes down to footlights and regards the audience. The others watch but don't speak. Hamlet clears his throat noisily and spits into the audience. A split second later he claps his hand to his eye and wipes himself. He goes back upstage.

Ros A compulsion towards philosophical introspection is his chief characteristic, if I may put it like that. It does not mean he is mad. It does not mean he isn't. Very often, it does not mean anything at all. Which may or may not be a kind of madness.

Guil It really boils down to symptoms. Pregnant replies, mystic allusions, mistaken identities, arguing his father is his mother, that sort of thing; intimations of suicide, forgoing of exercise, loss of mirth, hints of claustrophobia, not to say delusions of imprisonment; invocations of camels, chameleons, capons, whales, weasels, hawks, handsaws – riddles, quibbles and evasions; amnesia, paranoia, myopia; day-dreaming, hallucinations; stabbing his elders, abusing his parents, insulting his lover, and appearing hatless in public – knock-kneed, droop-stockinged and sighing like a love-sick schoolboy, which at his age is coming on a bit strong.

Ros And talking to himself.

Guil And talking to himself.

Ros and Guil move apart together.

Well, where has that got us?

Ros He's the Player.

Guil His play offended the King –

Ros – offended the King –

Guil – who orders his arrest –

Ros – orders his arrest –

Guil – so he escapes to England –

Ros On the boat to which he meets –

Guil Guildenstern and Rosencrantz taking Hamlet –

Ros – who also offended the King –

Guil – and killed Polonius –

Ros – offended the King in a variety of ways –

Guil – to England. (*Pause.*) That seems to be it.

Ros jumps up.

Ros Incidents! All we get is incidents! Dear God, is it too much to expect a little sustained action?!

And on the word, the Pirates attack. That is to say: Noise and shouts and rushing about. 'Pirates'.
   Everyone visible goes frantic. Hamlet draws his sword and rushes downstage. Guil, Ros and the Player draw swords and rush upstage. Collision. Hamlet turns back up. They turn back down. Collision. By which time there is general panic right upstage. All four charge upstage with Ros, Guil and the Player shouting:

At last!
To arms!
Pirates!
Up there!
Down there!
To my sword's length!
Action!

*All four reach the top, see something they don't like,
waver, run for their lives downstage:*

*Hamlet, in the lead, leaps into the left barrel. The
Player leaps into the right barrel. Ros and Guil leap into
the middle barrel. All closing the lids after them.*

*The lights dim to nothing while the sound of fighting
continues.*

The sound fades to nothing. The lights come up.

The middle barrel (Ros's and Guil's) is missing.

*The lid of the right-hand barrel is raised cautiously,
the heads of Ros and Guil appear.*

*The lid of the other barrel (Hamlet's) is raised. The
head of the Player appears.*

*All catch sight of each other and slam down lids.
Pause.*

Lids raised cautiously.

Ros (*relief*) They've gone. (*He starts to climb out*).That
was close. I've never thought quicker.

*They are all three out of barrels. Guil is wary and
nervous. Ros is light-headed. The Player is phlegmatic.
They note the missing barrel.
Ros looks round.*

Ros Where's –?

The Player takes off his hat in mourning.

Player Once more, alone – on our own resources.

Guil (*worried*) What do you mean? Where is he?

Player Gone.

Guil Gone where?

Player Yes, we were dead lucky there. If that's the word
I'm after.

Ros (*not a pick up*) Dead?

Player Lucky.

Ros (*he means*) Is he dead?

Player Who knows?

Guil (*rattled*) He's not coming back?

Player Hardly.

Ros He's dead then. He's dead as far as we're concerned.

Player Or we are as far as he is. (*He goes and sits on the floor to one side.*) Not too bad, is it?

Guil (*rattled*) But he can't – We're supposed to be – We've got a *letter* – We're going to England with a letter for the King –

Player Yes, that much seems certain. I congratulate you on the unambiguity of your situation.

Guil But you don't understand – it contains – we've had our instructions – The whole thing's pointless without him.

Player Pirates could happen to anyone. Just deliver the letter. They'll send ambassadors from England to explain . . .

Guil (*worked up*) Can't see – the pirates left us home and high – dry and home – drome – (*furiously*) The pirates left us high and dry!

Player (*comforting*) There . . .

Guil (*near tears*) Nothing will be resolved without him . . .

Player There . . . !

Guil We need Hamlet for our release!

Player There!

Guil What are we supposed to do?

Player This.

He turns away, lies down if he likes. Ros and Guil apart.

Ros Saved again.

Guil Saved for what?

Ros sighs.

Ros The sun's going down. (*Pause.*) It'll be night soon. (*Pause.*) If that's west. (*Pause.*) Unless we've –

Guil (*shouts*) Shut up! I'm sick of it! Do you think conversation is going to help us now?

Ros (*hurt, desperately ingratiating*) I – I bet you all the money I've got the year of my birth doubled is an odd number.

Guil (*moan*) No-o.

Ros *Your* birth!

Guil smashes him down.

Guil (*broken*) We've travelled too far, and our momentum has taken over; we move idly towards eternity, without possibility of reprieve or hope of explanation.

Ros Be happy – If you're not even *happy* what's so good about surviving? (*He picks himself up.*) We'll be all right. I suppose we just go on.

Guil Go where?

Ros To England.

Guil England! *That's* a dead end. I never believed in it anyway.

Ros All we've got to do is make our report and that'll be that. Surely.

Guil I don't *believe* it – A shore, a harbour, say – and we get off and we stop someone and say – Where's the King? – And he says, oh, you follow that road there and take the first left and – (*furiously*) I don't believe any of it!

Ros It doesn't sound very plausible.

Guil And even if we came face to face, what do we say?

Ros We say – We've arrived!

Guil (*kingly*) And who are you?

Ros We are Guildenstern and Rosencrantz.

Guil Which is which?

Ros Well, I'm – You're –

Guil What's it all about? –

Ros Well, we were bringing Hamlet – but then some pirates –

Guil I don't begin to understand. Who are all these people, what's it got to do with me? You turn up out of the blue with some cock and bull story –

Ros (*with letter*) We have a letter –

Guil (*snatches it, opens it*) A letter – yes – that's true. That's something . . . a letter . . . (*Reads*). 'As England is Denmark's faithful tributary . . . as love between them like the palm might flourish, etcetera . . . that on the knowing of this contents, without delay of any kind, should those bearers, Rosencrantz and Guildenstern, put to sudden death –'

> *He double takes. Ros snatches the letter. Guil snatches it back. Ros snatches it half back. They read it again and look up.*

The Player gets to his feet and walks over to his barrel and kicks it and shouts into it.

Player They've gone – It's all over!

One by one the Players emerge, impossibly, from the barrel, and form a casually menacing circle round Ros and Guil who are still appalled and mesmerised.

Guil (*quietly*) Where we went wrong was getting on a boat. We can move, of course, change direction, rattle about, but our movement is contained within a larger one that carries us along as inexorably as the wind and current . . .

Ros They had it in for us, didn't they? Right from the beginning. Who'd have thought that we were so important?

Guil But why? Was it all for this? Who are we that so much should converge on our little deaths? (*in anguish to the Player*) Who are *we*?

Player You are Rosencrantz and Guildenstern. That's enough.

Guil No – it is not enough. To be told so little – to such an end – and still, finally, to be denied an explanation . . .

Player In our experience, most things end in death.

Guil (*fear, vengeance, scorn*) Your experience? – *Actors!*

He snatches a dagger from the Player's belt and holds the point at the Player's throat: the Player backs and Guil advances, speaking more quietly.

I'm talking about death – and you've never experienced *that*. And you cannot *act* it. You die a thousand casual deaths – with none of that intensity which squeezes out life . . . and no blood runs cold anywhere. Because even as you die you know that you will come back in a different hat. But no one gets up after *death* – there is no applause – there is only silence and some second-hand clothes, and that's – *death* –

And he pushes the blade in up to the hilt. The Player stands with huge, terrible eyes, clutches at the wound as the blade withdraws: he makes small weeping sounds and falls to his knees, and then right down.

While he is dying, Guil, nervous, high, almost hysterical, wheels on the Tragedians –

If we have a destiny, then so had he – and if this is ours, then that was his – and if there are no explanations for us, then let there be none for him –

The Tragedians watch the Player die: they watch with some interest. The Player finally lies still. A short moment of silence. Then the Tragedians start to applaud with genuine admiration. The Player stands up, brushing himself down.

Player (*modestly*) Oh, come, come, gentlemen – no flattery – it was merely competent –

The Tragedians are still congratulating him. The Player approaches Guil, who stands rooted, holding the dagger.

What did you think? (*Pause.*) You see, it *is* the kind they do believe in – it's what is expected.

He holds his hand out for the dagger. Guil slowly puts the point of the dagger on to the Player's hand, and pushes . . . the blade slides back into the handle. The Player smiles, reclaims the dagger.

For a moment you thought I'd – cheated.

Ros relieves his own tension with loud nervy laughter.

Ros Oh, very good! *Very* good! Took me in completely –

didn't he take you in completely – (*Claps his hands.*) Encore! Encore!

Player (*activated, arms spread, the professional*) Deaths for all ages and occasions! Deaths by suspension, convulsion, consumption, incision, execution, asphyxiation and malnutrition –! Climactic carnage, by poison and by steel –! Double deaths by duel –! Show!

Alfred, still in his queen's costume, dies by poison: the Player, with rapier, kills the 'King' and duels with a fourth Tragedian, inflicting and receiving a wound: the two remaining Tragedians, the two 'Spies' dressed in the same coats as Ros and Guil, are stabbed, as before.
And the light is fading over the deaths which take place right upstage.
Dying amid the dying – tragically; romantically.

So there's an end to that – it's commonplace: light goes with life, and in the winter of your years the dark comes early . . .

Guil (*tired, drained, but still an edge of impatience; over the mime*) No . . . no . . . not for *us*, not like that. Dying is not romantic, and death is not a game which will soon be over . . . Death is not anything . . . death is not . . . It's the absence of presence, nothing more . . . the endless time of never coming back . . . a gap you can't see, and when the wind blows through it, it makes no sound . . .

The light has gone upstage. Only Guil and Ros are visible as Ros's clapping falters to silence.
Small pause.

Ros That's it, then, is it? (*No answer, he looks out front.*) The sun's going down. Or the earth's coming up, as the fashionable theory has it. (*Small pause.*) Not that it makes any difference. (*Pause.*) What was it all about? When did it begin? (*Pause, no answer.*) Couldn't we just stay put? I

mean no one is going to come on and drag us off . . .
They'll just have to wait. We're still young . . . fit . . .
we've got years . . . (*Pause. No answer.*) (*A cry*) We've
done nothing wrong! We didn't harm anyone. Did we?

Guil I can't remember.

Ros pulls himself together.

Ros All right, then. I don't care. I've had enough. To tell
you the truth, I'm relieved.

And he disappears from view.
Guil does not notice.

Guil Our names shouted in a certain dawn . . . a message
. . . a summons . . . there must have been a moment, at
the beginning, where we could have said – no. But
somehow we missed it. (*He looks round and sees he is
alone.*) Rosen – ? Guil – ? (*He gathers himself.*) Well, we'll
know better next time. Now you see me, now you –

And disappears.
*Immediately the whole stage is lit up, revealing,
upstage, arranged in the approximate positions last held
by the dead Tragedians, the tableau of court and
corpses which is the last scene of Hamlet.*
*That is: The King, Queen, Laertes and Hamlet all
dead. Horatio holds Hamlet. Fortinbras is there.*
So are two **Ambassadors** *from England.*

Ambassador The sight is dismal;
And our affairs from England come too late.
The ears are senseless that should give us hearing
To tell him his commandment is fulfilled,
That Rosencrantz and Guildenstern are dead.
Where should we have our thanks?

Horatio Not from his mouth,
Had it the ability of life to thank you:

117

He never gave commandment for their death.
But since, so jump upon this bloody question,
You from the Polack wars, and you from England,
Are here arrived, give order that these bodies
High on a stage be placed to the view;
And let me speak to the yet unknowing world
How these things came about: so shall you hear
Of carnal, bloody and unnatural acts,
Of accidental judgments, casual slaughters,
Of deaths put on by cunning and forced cause,
And, in this upshot, purposes mistook
Fallen on the inventors' heads: all this can I
Truly deliver.

> *But during the above speech the play fades, overtaken*
> *by dark and music.*